Ste
hen Crane's The red badge of
age / .

8065139652
$30.00 ocm76064586

UL 19 2007

Bloom's

GUIDES

Stephen Crane's
The Red Badge of Courage

CURRENTLY AVAILABLE

The Adventures of Huckleberry Finn
All the Pretty Horses
Animal Farm
Beloved
Beowulf
Brave New World
The Catcher in the Rye
The Chosen
The Crucible
Cry, the Beloved Country
Death of a Salesman
Fahrenheit 451
Frankenstein
The Glass Menagerie
The Grapes of Wrath
Great Expectations
The Great Gatsby
Hamlet
The Handmaid's Tale
The House on Mango Street
I Know Why the Caged Bird Sings
The Iliad
Jane Eyre

Lord of the Flies
Macbeth
Maggie: A Girl of the Streets
The Member of the Wedding
The Metamorphosis
Native Son
Of Mice and Men
1984
The Odyssey
Oedipus Rex
One Hundred Years of Solitude
Pride and Prejudice
Ragtime
The Red Badge of Courage
Romeo and Juliet
Slaughterhouse-Five
The Scarlet Letter
Snow Falling on Cedars
A Streetcar Named Desire
The Sun Also Rises
A Tale of Two Cities
The Things They Carried
To Kill a Mockingbird
The Waste Land

Bloom's

GUIDES

Stephen Crane's
The Red Badge
of Courage

Edited & with an Introduction
by Harold Bloom

BLOOM'S
LITERARY CRITICISM
An imprint of Infobase Publishing

Bloom's Guides: The Red Badge of Courage

Copyright © 2007 by Infobase Publishing
Introduction © 2007 by Harold Bloom

Bloom's Literary Criticism
An imprint of Infobase Publishing
132 West 31st Street
New York NY 10001

ISBN-10: 0-7910-9367-0
ISBN-13: 978-0-7910-9367-2

Library of Congress Cataloging-in-Publication Data
Stephen Crane's The red badge of courage / Harold Bloom, editor.
    p. cm. -- (Bloom's guides)
  Includes bibliographical references (p.   ) and index.
  ISBN 0-7910-9367-0 (hardcover)
  1. Crane, Stephen, 1871-1900. Red badge of courage. 2. United
States--History--Civil War, 1861-1865--Literature and the war.
I. Bloom, Harold. II. Title: The red badge of courage. III. Series.
  PS1449.C85R397 2007
  813'.4--dc22   2006036786

Contributing Editor: Gabriel Welsch
Cover design by Takeshi Takahashi
Printed in the United States of America
Bang EJB 10 9 8 7 6 5 4 3 2 1

Contents

Introduction

HAROLD BLOOM

For an American reader in 2007, over a full century after the first publication of *The Red Badge of Courage*, Stephen Crane's short novel is likely to seem far less original than it was and still is. Our novelists of war—Ernest Hemingway and Norman Mailer in particular—absorbed Crane's impressionistic mode of rendering battle, Hemingway directly from Crane, Mailer through Hemingway. Impressionism in *The Red Badge of Courage* has little to do with Impressionist painting, though H.G. Wells affirmed that Crane was more like the expatriate American painter, Whistler, than he was like Tolstoy or Joseph Conrad. Style in Crane's writing is an art of omission, even of the names of his protagonists, so long as he can delay divulging them. The central figure, the Young Soldier, later named as Henry Fleming, is a lens or camera eye whose perceptions and sensations provide all the material that is available to the third-person narrator, who presumably is Stephen Crane himself. We therefore are not given a coherent account of the bloody Civil War battle of Chancellorsville (2–4 May, 1863). You would not know from reading *The Red Badge of Courage* that Robert E. Lee's army won the battle, at the cost of a fatal wound to Stonewall Jackson. Chancellorsville was the last major victory for the Confederacy, and tempted Lee to his invasion of Pennsylvania that ended with the disaster of Pickett's charge at Gettysburg. But none of that is Crane's concern in his impressionistic novel. Like his mentor Tolstoy, Crane knows that battle is a blur to the individual who perceives it. In *War and Peace*, Tolstoy's Pierre observes the crucial, vast fight at Borodino between Napoleon and the Russians, and sees only a senseless chaos. Crane's Henry Fleming also sees only a heap of broken images, fragments of perception, sudden sensations of fear or grotesque visions of a distorted phantasmagoria.

The mind of Henry Fleming, and not the battlefield of Chancellorsville, is the scene of the book, but Fleming's mind is not Crane's subject in the sense that the mind of Hamlet is Shakespeare's. Hamlet's mind is intellectual to the highest degree; his tragedy is the tragedy of thought, of thinking not too much but too well. Henry Fleming's consciousness is painted for us, rather than thought through. Hamlet's intellectual capacities, immense to begin with, grow to infinitude. Henry Fleming, who begins with a limited vision of reality, unable always to distinguish between his perceptions and outer actualities, develops into someone who can trust his own visual impressions. In the context of battle and its fears, such trust is all-important. Whether Fleming, at the close, has evolved into a person of considerable courage, Crane leaves somewhat unclear. Whatever Crane's intentions, the irony of his style continues: "He had been to touch the great death, and found that, after all, it was but the great death. He was a man." I once rephrased that as: "He had been to touch the great fear, and found that, after all, it was still the great fear. He was not yet a man." Which is to say that, the fear of being afraid dehumanizes one, but to accept one's own mortality joins one with one's comrades. Such a joining with others restores the sense of humanity that makes Fleming one of us, all condemned men and women but with a kind of indefinite reprieve. Crane does not wish us to see Fleming as a potential war hero or even as a survivor. The Young Soldier is an Everyman, making a pilgrim's progress into reality, and the name of the reality principle is the necessity of dying.

Henry Fleming, when we last see him, has raised himself to the fury of battle, but still lacks the self-possession of Jim Conklin, the perhaps Christ-like figure of heroism who truly wears the red badge of courage. Fleming's fury, which sustains him in battle, is hardly Crane's conception of courage. Clearsightedness is; Henry is both angry and visually perceptive at the close, which is evidently an ambiguity that the always-ironic Crane sought to establish. For Crane, consistency is impossible, whether in battle or in ordinary life. Heroism is possible, but is bound to be confused with rage, and cannot persist even as a level perception of reality. Crane was so pervasive an ironist that he did not exempt himself as writer from the dilemmas of fear and courage shading into one another. The author's stance in *The Red Badge of Courage* strives for a detachment that Crane knows he cannot attain. In this regard, Crane is closer to Norman Mailer than to Hemingway, who invested himself in the beautiful detachment of his prose, and sometimes deceived himself into believing that he had reached a Tolstoyan eminence of being able to render the completeness of ordinary reality. Crane seems to have known better; the Impressionism of *The Red Badge of Courage* is not so much an ambitious attempt at modern epic as it is an honest acceptance of Crane's limitations. He was too aware of his own mortality to escape an ironic stance; tubercular, he died at twenty-eight, just five years after *The Red Badge of Courage* was published. Readers tend to agree that the book's permanent greatness has more to do with its clearsightedness than with its ironies.

Biographical Sketch

Born in 1871 in Newark, New Jersey, Stephen Crane was the fourteenth child of Reverend Dr. Jonathan Townley Crane, a Methodist minister, and Mary Helen Peck Crane, whom John Berryman termed "a madly missionary woman." While his father preached, his mother deplored, in written tracts published in newspapers and by pamphleteers, such excess as dancing, card playing, drinking, and frequenting billiard rooms. By Crane's own accounting, however, the missionary zeal of the family ebbed by the time he was in his teens. Still, he rebelled against religion and his being the son of a clergyman, and the adventuresome rebelliousness stayed with him throughout his short life.

He attended both Lafayette College (in 1890) and Syracuse University (in 1891), though he spent more time with baseball, poker, boxing, and shooting pool than with studies. Crane's associates in the pool halls did talk of writers, in particular Tolstoy and Flaubert, but a friend of Crane's, John Barry, once noted that "Crane at 21 was woefully ignorant of books. Indeed, he deliberately avoided reading from a fear of being influenced by other writers."

Crane did not earn a degree from either institution, though he was active in athletics and did join a fraternity. He would have stayed at Lafayette had his brother, Townley, not recommended him for a position with the *New York Tribune*, as a correspondent in Syracuse. However, the job also practically ensured Crane would not do well. He spent his time writing stories for the *Tribune*, as well as for other periodicals, and making the varsity baseball team. While his interest in literature remained (he gave two lectures on the topic to members of his fraternity while at Syracuse), he also felt that the most compelling place to be was the courthouse, which he had found through his reporting chores. He spent so much time there, on the baseball field, and in other pursuits that he failed at his studies (having ceased attending classes altogether by the spring of 1891) and was asked to leave Syracuse that June.

Crane knew he wanted to write, and felt strongly that a writer should be able to write about anything, as long as he could observe it and develop something interesting to say. Like many writers, he also knew that he wanted to live in New York City, to feed on the observable and to make a living with the pen in one of the few places in the country where it could be done. The living, however, was not grand. Crane lived in New York's infamous Bowery, home to derelicts, prostitutes, and writers and artists. Crane himself habituated the prototypical writer's garret, living with several painters and bohemians, a group he termed "The Indians," in a loft. While he held a job for a time as a reporter for the *New York Herald*, by late winter of 1892, he was getting by entirely as a freelancer, selling articles to New York papers and magazines. As he did so, he wrote a series of pieces about life in the Bowery, as well as his first novel, *Maggie: A Girl of the Streets*.

Maggie was a frank and realistic novel that dealt with the brutalities of Bowery life, particularly prostitution. At a time when genteel and sentimental romances and faraway swashbuckling tales were the staples of readers' diets, American publishers felt such a "shocking" book would not sell and, further, would scandalize them. Having no luck with publishers, Crane prevailed on another of his brothers, William, for a loan so he might pay to have the book published and sold cheaply at newsstands and on magazine racks. It didn't work. The book was a failure, and the majority of the print run was stored in William's attic.

In 1892, Crane became associated with Hamlin Garland, an established writer at the time. Crane gave Garland a copy of *Maggie*, which Garland then gave to William Dean Howells, one of the most important figures in the movement toward literary realism in American writing. Impressed, Howells threw his support behind Crane, and though it still did not result in a major publisher picking up *Maggie*, it did lead to Crane selling some of his Bowery sketches, and starting to develop his reputation. Money came in, and he was no longer quite as destitute, though he continued to live with "The Indians" in the Bowery.

Crane grew tired of living in squalor and fighting for meals. While the stories had brought some money, as did occasional handouts from family members, and patronage from Howells and Garland, Crane's existence remained decidedly hand-to-mouth. Wanting to make money, Crane embarked on writing a crowd-pleasing war story in the tradition of the popular romantic works of the time. However, his wish to write honestly gripped him, and the work became *The Red Badge of Courage*.

Crane wrote the book surrounded by people who would have a profound impact on his style. Several scholars have pointed out that among "The Indians" were a number of painters attempting to build on what the Impressionists were accomplishing on canvas in Europe. Several suspect that the impressionistic techniques that fire and render distinct Crane's natural realism came from watching his roommates work on their paintings.

Many scholars think Howells introduced Crane to the poems of Emily Dickinson, which Crane claimed as the inspiration for the grim, terse pieces that comprised *The Black Riders and Other Lines*, published in 1895, just before *Red Badge*. Others have noted that Dickinson's outlook may well have helped Crane refine his own worldview, and might have been critical to the pervasive dread and the ambiguous ending that faced Henry Fleming.

Through early 1895, Crane made a weeks-long train excursion through the West, under assignment for the Bacheller Syndicate (the syndicate that would later agree to serialize *Red Badge*). He had gone to do stories in St. Louis, New Orleans, Nebraska, Mexico, Arizona, and Nevada, more of the kinds of sketches that he had successfully sold to other magazines. The editors had wanted him to find "new color" in the American West, a place that, although its frontier and cowboy days were long over, still held that mystique for eastern readers. While in Nebraska to write about the drought, he met Willa Cather and discussed *Red Badge* with her, while he awaited word from a publisher, D. Appleton and Company, on whether it would take the book. At the same time, his book of verse was being produced.

Appleton sent Crane a contract to publish *Red Badge*, which the author signed in June 1895. While the novel was set to appear in October, Bacheller arranged to have it published in a significantly abridged form in hundreds of newspapers around the country, making Crane an instant celebrity. The appearance of the full version won Stephen Crane accolades on both sides of the Atlantic, ensuring the writer would not be poor again.

However, Crane's health would deteriorate over the next several years, exacerbated by personal troubles and a travel schedule that would have laid low many fit individuals, much less a sickly man who had endured years of living in squalor. Through 1896, he became involved with a number of women, most famously Nellie Crouse, to whom he wrote scores of letters that have since been published in a collection. The letters provide insight to his ideas; he once wrote to her and characterized life as "labor and sorrow. I do not confront it blithely. I confront it with desperate resolution. There is not even much hope in my attitude.... It is not a fine prospect." He was also still covering life in the Bowery and other squalid locales in the city for the Hearst papers. While in the Tenderloin district "studying human nature," as he put it, Crane infamously rushed to the defense of Dora Clark, a woman arrested on what Crane believed to be trumped-up charges of solicitation. His battle on her behalf resulted in newspaper coverage that made him look, at best, foolhardy and, at worse, immoral.

The same year, he published two more novels, neither of which did well or approached the artistic levels of *Maggie* or *Red Badge*. By year's end, Crane had gone to Jacksonville, Florida, to report on the war with Cuba, as the city had become a main location for arms smuggling and other illicit activity. While there, he met Cora Taylor, whom biographer Linda H. Davis characterized as "proprietress of the finest bawdy house in Jacksonville, the Hotel de Dream." Taylor was urbane, sophisticated, and worldly, and Crane was smitten. By most accounts, the two were devoted, even if some individuals felt Cora did not quite measure up to Crane, or that she was somehow eclipsed by him. Crane evidently did not feel that way. He took great pains to take care of her; Taylor became his common-law wife and, on his death a few years later, the sole beneficiary of his estate.

In early 1897, Crane was a passenger aboard a boat that sank off the coast of Florida. For days, Crane was thought to have died, and newspapers around the country reported of his drowning. But the author survived in a dinghy and later wrote a fictionalized account of the experience, resulting in his most enduring short story, "The Open Boat." He traveled to Greece as a correspondent covering the Greco-Turkish War later in 1897, and then traveled to England with Cora. He and Cora made a residence in England in a run down manor house. While there, he began a friendship of mutual admiration with the novelists Joseph Conrad, Henry James, and H.G. Wells. In 1898, Crane returned briefly to the United States at the outbreak of the Spanish-American War. While he volunteered for service, he was denied entrance to the military due to his exhibiting symptoms of tuberculosis. Instead, he went to Cuba as a war correspondent.

His correspondence experiences drove some of his last works. The stint in Greece provided him the grist for his novel *Active Service*, and his dispatches from Cuba were later collected and published posthumously as *Wounds in the Rain*. From all his war experiences came a volume of verse, *War Is Kind*, published in 1899. At the same time as the war writings were appearing, his short stories and sketches produced two volumes; *The Open Boat and Other Tales of Adventure* appeared in 1898, and *Whilomville Stories* in 1900.

Illness caused Crane to return from Cuba in 1898, and by 1899, tuberculosis had made him quite sick. Late in 1899, the disease had so worsened that Cora decided to take her husband to a sanitarium in Germany's Black Forest, in hopes of stemming the worsening of Crane's health. It did not work, and complications from tuberculosis ended Crane's life in June 1900, at age 28.

The Story Behind the Story

Stephen Crane was a journalist and dedicated himself to chronicling squalor and then war. His zeal for chronicling experience also met with his rather severe requirement (for a writer) that he actually experience that about which he tried to write.

He once noted in a letter, "You can tell nothing ... unless you are in that condition yourself." At the time, he lived in the Bowery and wrote about squalor, so had, perhaps, the moral authority to stand by his words. However, when he wrote *The Red Badge of Courage* and published it in 1895, at the age of 25, its subject matter a baptism of fire at the Battle of Chancellorsville during the American Civil War, he broke his own rule. He was not, himself, born until almost eight years after Chancellorsville, five years into Reconstruction, and even once of age, he never held a rifle in service to his country.

That said, Crane's high school education came from a military school, where he was reported to have excelled as a student, athlete, and social personality. The military training was important as well; by several accounts, he was quite handy with a firearm. But military exercises, as Henry Fleming realizes, are no substitute for the experience of battle.

However, Crane would not see battle prior to his writing his most famous book. He tried to enlist, but even then, his childhood illnesses made it so that he was deemed too weak for service, and was turned away for health reasons.

In place of battle experiences, Crane cobbled together other experiences to help make realistic Henry Fleming's battle experiences. While at Claverack College, Crane was the student of a Civil War veteran who had served in a regiment in New York that had suffered bad casualties at Antietam. The professor, a retired general, was very popular among students and frequently shared his stories of war with young men in his charge.

Working as a journalist for his brother Townley, Crane met down-and-out individuals, circus performers, and the gamblers and showgirls of Atlantic City. He thus became well-acquainted with a variety of people of different means and experiences. His journalistic work continued even as he went from Lafayette College to Syracuse University to the Bowery.

He knew of exposure to the elements; as Bernard Oldsey has pointed out, Crane was once so desperate for cash that, lacking even the wherewithal to catch a train, he walked, in winter, through mud and frost, to his brother William's house, in New Jersey. Delirious with fatigue, Crane only vaguely recalled a stranger coming to him, taking his arm, and helping him to his brother's home. Many critics have pointed out how the experience mirrors the content and spirit of chapter 7 of *Red Badge*.

Another of Crane's brothers, Edmund, was a Civil War enthusiast, historian, and expert on Chancellorsville. Critics note this association as the likely reason for the book's setting.

Finally, Crane read widely, and many note the influence of two other important writers on war, Zola and Tolstoy—particularly their novels *Sevastopol* (Tolstoy) and *La Débâcle* (Zola).

Still, in spite of all the available influences and Crane's clear career as a journalist, military men of the time, in particular a group of professional soldiers in England, were shocked to discover that Stephen Crane was hardly more than a boy, that he had never seen battle, and yet had written a psychologically accurate portrayal of war. To Crane's credit, he later acted as a war correspondent, covering the Greco-Turkish War and the Spanish-American War, both assignments done after the novel was published. Crane had taken the assignments, in part, to satisfy for himself that his portrayal was as accurate as others claimed it to be.

That Stephen Crane wrote such a stirring book, that it was respected for its commitment to realism, and that its verisimilitude made readers feel they were hearing from a veteran are all testimony to the power of invention that a talented and determined writer can achieve. Crane never saw battle as a soldier, and only later saw it as a journalist. In fact, his bohemian lifestyle during the years he wrote *Red Badge* was downright antithetical to the values the military did and still does profess. Even so, his experiences provided the raw emotional and physical materials of experience so that he could imagine war in such a way as to earn the approving nods of veterans.

List of Characters

Henry Fleming: the youth leaves home in a fit of heroic visions and enlists in the Union Army. The novel opens with him waiting, with his regiment, for the battle plans of the generals to send them on to fight. His visions of valor are tested and broken in the battle chronicled in the novel, and after what he regards as initial success (he blindly fights, too frozen to desert), he flees after a second push by Confederate forces. He rejoins his company after a search through the woods, and as he does so, finds in himself a measure of valor as he fights again. Throughout the novel, his mental state reels from solipsistic hero fantasies to deep self-loathing and rebuke, and his actions are fevered attempts to change or capitalize on an emotional state. By the novel's end, he is satisfied with his ability to fight and stand his ground, even though he is bothered by the fact of his desertion. As he marches on to the next battle, he has changed, but it is also clear that he has learned very little about war, human character, bravery, or the world.

Jim Conklin: the tall soldier gently accepts the difficulties thrust upon him. As other soldiers complain, Jim elicits admiration from the other men as he considers, often philosophically, the reasons for actions, decisions, and so on. He reminds the others to accept their circumstances. Just as his shirt is compared early on to a banner, so, too, is Jim a kind of standard, a rallying point for the men and an inspiration for Henry. His death is prolonged, impressionistic, laborious, and almost ritualistic. He dies for the suffering of others, and as such awakens Henry to the costs and seriousness of the battles in which he is engaged, such that many have argued Conklin is a Christ figure in the novel.

Wilson: the loud soldier brags to others and heckles Henry at the novel's outset. However, once Henry finds his way back to the unit after being separated in battle, Wilson comes to his aid. Henry notes that Wilson is humble, caring, and changed from immersion in battle and familiarity with mortality. Wilson and Henry change together through the events of the battle that follows, and together fight valiantly (by Henry's estimation, as well as that of the others, most notably the lieutenant).

Summary and Analysis

Joseph Conrad captures the crux of Henry Fleming's dilemma in an essay he wrote some 30 years after the book's first appearance. Conrad wrote that Crane's character stands before an archetypal challenge: "He stands before the unknown. He would like to prove to himself by some reasoning process that he will not 'run from the battle.' And in his unblooded regiment he can find no help. He is alone with the problem of courage." The novel, thus, is not a war story, per se; it is a story that has at its core the common characteristic of so many great works: what William Faulkner called "the human heart in conflict with itself." For Crane, the additional point is that the human heart is no more special or particular or sober, perhaps, than other forces of nature.

Stephen Crane's masterpiece, *The Red Badge of Courage*, opens with a paragraph portraying the army as a living thing, "stretched out on the hills, resting." As the animal awakens, the scene also takes on color. With those two stylistic choices, so begins a novel that, in 1895, largely through its author's use of such bold and distinctive (for his day) techniques, effectively changed how war stories were told and, according to many critics, ushered in the beginning of modern literature.

The early likening of the army to an animal is the first of many instances where Crane uses animal imagery to make authorial statements about humans, about the army itself, about nature, and about war. At the same time, Crane's color use begins another device he will employ throughout the novel as a pathetic fallacy.

Crane starts from a narrative vantage that takes in the entirety of the scene, but does so without naming the place (or, later, the battle). He does so, as Lee Clark Mitchell points out, to approximate how soldiers themselves would have experienced the war. The battles had not yet lent place names any significance; woods and streams were the backyards of people who lived great distances from where the soldiers themselves called home. The wilderness was not yet ordered by history, and to the soldiers, was still simply wilderness, with its beauty, mystery, and potential horrors intact.

At the same time, Crane is able to use the psychic distance achieved at the outset to swoop in and offer a panoramic view of the army as a beast and nature as, initially, malevolent. The camp fires gain hostility from their association with the "low brows" of the hills, and the river is "sorrowful blackness."

Into the malevolence and uncertainty runs an unnamed soldier, waving his shirt "bannerlike," acting as a standard-bearer. He comes with news as well, though Crane's writing that the soldier had heard the tale "from a reliable friend, who had heard it from a truthful cavalryman" and so on undercuts the soldier's veracity. When readers later learn the soldier is the redoubtable Jim Conklin, it is not Conklin's honesty that is called into question, but whether or not the army itself is reliable.

Conklin tells of the army's plans to move, to attack, and while he is greeted with derision, one "youthful private" hopes Conklin's words are true. The youthful private is Henry Fleming, the novel's protagonist. Crane introduces Fleming so that readers see the young man daydreaming about the glories of battle. Fleming had dreamt of war "all his life—of vague and bloody conflicts that thrilled him with their sweep and fire." But he also suspects that the days of glorious engagements are gone. The evidence of what he sees as his army's dithering supports his assumption that "Men were better, or more timid. Secular and religious education had effaced the throat-grappling instinct, or else firm finance held in check the passions."

At the time Crane wrote the novel, however, his contemporary writers and thinkers were very much concerned with brutality as it existed for freed slaves, vast legions of laborers (regardless of race), as well as the brutality of industrialization's economic system. But Henry Fleming might well have come by his idealism honestly; such ideas could be found in popular romantic stories and in sentimental and nationalistic propaganda. Fleming seems youthful and almost unbelievably naïve to modern readers, but he would have had access only to very sentimental paintings of armed conflict, or to highly melodramatic stories. Photography was still nascent, and journalism, while practiced in cities, likely would not have made it out to the rural Fleming farm.

Filled with ideas because "tales of great movements shook the land," Fleming had burned to enlist. The only voice he heard urging him not to enlist came from his mother. For Crane, Fleming's mother represents an experienced, hometown morality. In some manuscript drafts of the novel, in fact, Crane made her more overtly religious. In the version published by Appleton in 1895, and seen now as the definitive version of what Crane intended, the mother's attitude comes across most forcefully as that of a mother looking out for what is really only a boy. She talks of his socks, warns him of the corrupting forces of the army, and, finally, warns him that he "must never do no shirking, child, on my account. If so be a time comes when yeh have to be kilt or do a mean thing, why, Henry, don't think of anything 'cept what's right, because there's many a woman has to bear up 'ginst such things these times, and the Lord'll take keer of us all." The religious base for her morality is still present, but the care she exhibits has more to do with being a mother than with being a believer.

For the youth, her speech is irritating. It is only when he considers her speech in retrospect that he feels "suddenly ashamed of his purposes." He remembers how he had once had a higher calling, having been seminary trained, but that shame quickly dissipates as he begins to feel a superiority to his former classmates, those who had not come to the war. As he does so, he begins to lament that he had not yet been tested by severe situations; "he was an unknown quantity."

As he worries how he will hold up in battle, Jim Conklin and the loud soldier enter the tent and begin wrangling as to whether the regiment will or will not actually see fighting the next day. As they fight, Fleming interjects and asks, "How do you think the reg'ment'll do? . . . Think any of the boys'll run?" Conklin says he suspects some will, and reveals that everyone worries about such things, and that even if people run at first, they come back and fight again. To Fleming, the words make him feel "gratitude" for the wise perspective of the tall soldier. "He now was in a measure reassured."

In **chapter 2** we learn that the army did not fight. Conklin had been "the fast-flying messenger of a mistake." For Fleming, the delay is maddening. He needs the fight so that he can take some measure of himself; "he fretted for an opportunity."

In Conklin, Fleming sees "serene unconcern" and how it provides the tall soldier "a measure of confidence." While Conklin is, in this way, reassuring, Fleming longs for "another who suspected himself. A sympathetic comparison of mental notes would have been a joy to him."

The regiment languishes in camp for days, and doubt gnaws at the young private. He tries to find among his fellow soldiers someone who has the same worries, but is too afraid to state his own fears, and so cannot find another with whom he can commiserate. He worries alternately that all the other soldiers are heroes waiting to happen, and at other times that they are all bravado, all "liars" yet to be exposed in battle. The thoughts make him disgusted with himself.

Then, one morning:

> He found himself in the ranks of his prepared regiment. The men were whispering speculations and recounting old rumors. In the gloom before the break of the day their uniforms glowed a deep purple hue. From across the river the red eyes were still peering. In the eastern sky there was a yellow patch like a rug laid for the feet of the coming sun; and against it, black and patternlike, loomed the gigantic figure of the colonel on a gigantic horse.

The description is a very good example of an aspect of Crane's technique that has attracted a great deal of critical attention. *The Red Badge of Courage* is replete with color use, and Crane decisively uses those color references to comment on mood, ideas, and the action of the book. As David Halliburton notes in *The Color of the Sky*, "Only with difficulty, and at the risk of fudging, can Crane's famous colors be categorized neatly." His remark refers to considering color and Crane's use of it throughout his novels, stories, and poems. In reading *Red Badge*, though, Crane's impressionistic use of primary and secondary colors is relatively consistent, and worth interpreting.

In the paragraph excerpted above, the uniforms become purple. They are Union uniforms, and so are actually a deep navy blue. Given how Crane throughout uses the color red in reference to war, battle, violence, and rage, it is significant that the purple of the uniforms can be read as a mix of the blue of the army itself (a color suggesting righteousness, as in the "vast blue demonstration" of chapter 1) mixing with the red of battle, or its imminence.

Black signifies distance, remove, uncaring, and even monstrousness. It is reserved for the river, the dark woods from which come the red fires of the enemy, or the shadowy officers whose callousness for the men Fleming resents.

White, used sparely, is comfort, domesticity, purity. His tent wall is white, as is the flag, in parts.

Yellow is also used and often describes either the sky or artillery, but it also suggests sickliness throughout the novel. Thus, the color is pestilential, warding. The patch laid for the feet is, as Halliburton notes, "homely," but it is also sickly, the sign of a dawn coming that has savagery to come with it.

Or so the men think. The events of the day result only in marching and maneuvering, and at one point a young girl standing up to a fat soldier who attempts to pilfer her horse. By nightfall the regiment camps again, and while the youth is frustrated at another lack of action, the menace of the chapter's opening remains, in the red fires, in the red shadows of his tent as he continues to worry how he will fare in battle.

Chapter 3 opens with more of Crane's foreshadowing use of color. The river is "wine-tinted" by fire, and the "sudden gleams of silver or gold" suggest that Fleming might be on the verge of glory. Crane tends to use the colors of the precious metals to signify something on a higher plane than typical existence. The greatest deeds yield gold, the greatest valor is silver. For instance, when describing the still-green character of the regiment, Crane notes that the regiment's headgear reflected a lack of experience; "there were no letters of faded gold speaking from the colors."

The regiment marches once more, only to once again camp at nightfall having seen no fighting. Fleming is not the only frustrated soldier; several of the men are counting the miles, complaining about rations, and dumping excess gear they see no need to carry. Conklin, wise beyond his experiences, encourages Fleming to drop unnecessary clothing and sacks. He says, "You can now eat and shoot ... That's all you want to do."

On a "gray" dawn—the color of Confederate soldiers, grim portents, and suffering—Conklin kicks Fleming in the leg to waken him and the regiment lurches toward skirmishers. The mass movement is disorienting, and Fleming is seized by self-doubt and the realization of his own helplessness in the face of the war machine:

> He was bewildered. As he ran with his comrades he strenuously tried to think, but all he knew was that if he fell down those coming behind would tread upon him. All his faculties seemed to be needed to guide him over and past obstructions. He felt carried along by a mob.
>
> The sun spread disclosing rays, and, one by one, regiments burst into view like armed men just born of the earth. The youth perceived that the time had come. He was about to be measured. For a moment he felt in the face of his great trial like a babe, and the flesh over his heart seemed very thin. He seized time to look about him calculatingly.
>
> But he instantly saw that it would be impossible for him to escape from the regiment. It inclosed [sic] him. And there were iron laws of tradition and law on four sides. He was in a moving box.

Crane reveals Fleming's immaturity as the youth immediately feels that he had not signed up for the army of his own free will. "He had been dragged by the merciless government. And now they were taking him out to be slaughtered." But in the very next paragraph, spurred forward by an "impulse of curiosity," Fleming hastens up a hill, expecting a battle scene.

As an author, Crane does not provide any authorial intervention or commentary regarding Fleming. Rather, Crane simply allows the reader access to all of Fleming's thoughts, without revealing which of those thoughts are "better" or more sound. William Dean Howells had commented that Crane's earlier work, *Maggie: A Girl of the Streets*, was a success due to its "utter lack of style." Such an exclamation was not an insult. At the time Crane was writing, popular stories and novels would have had a great deal of interjection from the author. A different writer at the time might have handled the scene by intoning, "Young Fleming was but a boy, dear reader, and one ill-equipped to handle the crushing burdens Providence had laid upon his shoulders." Instead, Crane puts Fleming's thoughts on the page, good and bad, in the order they arrive, showing readers the range of psychological experience the youth undergoes in both the mundane hunch of marching and camping and in the heat of the battle. Crane was nearly alone in using such a technique at the time he wrote; for that reason, he also won praise for *Red Badge* as an early example of a "psychological" novel.

As Fleming tries to observe all that is happening in the skirmish, he stumbles upon a dead soldier in "an awkward suit of yellowish brown." The color is again associated with decay and illness. The man's presence does not deter the regiment, that "opened covertly to avoid the corpse." The corpse is an omen of what awaits them, and for Fleming is attractive, that he might "walk around the body and stare; the impulse of the living to try and read in the dead eyes the answer to the Question."

He begins to worry that the regiment is marching into a trap of sorts, that the woods and vales hid "fierce-eyed hosts," and that it was his job, as an enlightened soldier, to warn them all. The generals were "stupids" and "idiots," and his urge to shout "shrill and passionate words" nearly overtakes him. He looks around the men near him and notices "expressions of deep interest" and then realizes "they were going to look at war, the red animal—war, the blood-swollen god." Crane's characterization of war as vicious, animalistic, and primal contrasted with the typical Victorian mythological treatment of battles, and certainly differed with what Fleming would have read in newspaper coverage, had the youth had access to a newspaper.

Fleming fears speaking out, lest he be mocked, and as he is stricken and wandering, the lieutenant of his company goads him on, saying "no skulking'll do here." Fleming "mended his pace with suitable haste. And he hated the lieutenant, who had no appreciation of fine minds, He was a mere brute." Thus, insulted, worried about the trap, worrying whether he will fight or run, and then enveloped in rifle smoke and noise, and the "cathedral light" of the forest, Fleming is astounded when, on the verge of battle, the regiment is ordered to stand down and withdraw.

Fleming grows angry, petulant, and expresses his disgust to Conklin. Conklin, "with calm faith," began a "heavy explanation." Conklin's taking on the burden of the generals with a young soldier is another manner in which he redeems the army.

As Fleming continues, Conklin, "philosophical" says, "Oh, I suppose we must go reconnoitering around the country jest to keep 'em from getting too close, or to develop 'em, or something." His explanation, again, takes the forgiving stance of assuming wisdom and motive where, to those suffering, there appears to be none. He lets them know the generals (or the war god, perhaps) work in mysterious ways, so to speak.

While Fleming complains, Conklin is patient. But when Wilson, the loud soldier, complains, Conklin yells at him, calls him a "little fool. You little damn cuss." No reason is given for Conklin's differing treatment of Wilson, but Crane does describe how Conklin grows "quiet and contented" as he eats, as though the food were an offering, as though his "spirit seemed then to be communing with the viands." He is a calm presence, bearing tribulations with dignity. He is a redeeming presence, which has led many scholars to draw parallels between Jim Conklin's moral importance to war and the soldiers and what Christians believe is Jesus Christ's message of forgiveness and redemption.

The chapter ends with the soldiers again preparing to see battle, and the brigade ahead of Fleming's regiment runs forward toward the din. Fleming's regiment is to go next. As they wait to go, the loud soldier approaches Fleming and hands him "a little packet done up in a yellow envelope." Again, the color represents sickliness and failure, and in this instance, it is a failure of character; his lip is "girlish," and his maudlin fear of death and his wish for Henry to bring the note to "his folks" elicits revulsion from Fleming. He is appalled at Wilson's show of cowardice, at how his request "ended in a quavering sob of pity for himself." Even as Fleming protests, "the other gave him a glance as from the depths of the tomb."

Chapter 4 opens with men again speculating on what has happened in the battle so far and what will happen. Crane presents the snippets of dialogue without attribution, as if they had simply bubbled up to the ears of the reader, just as they would have to soldiers overhearing conversations as they walked.

The sounds and descriptions that follow the opening snippets reveal chaos and violence. A flag tosses "in the smoke, angrily," and men are a "turbulent stream" coming across a field. A battery moves "at a frantic gallop," and a shell "screaming like a storm banshee" flies over the soldiers and lands, "exploding redly." Fleming sees the lieutenant get shot in the hand.

The lieutenant's injury is not glorious, but almost random. It is also mundane. Gone are Fleming's airs about glorious "eagle-eyed" stares and protections and all other manner of gallantry. The injury to the lieutenant comes from a musket ball that could have killed him, but didn't. Instead, the injury is almost comic:

He began to swear so wondrously that a nervous laugh went along the regimental line. The officer's profanity sounded conventional. It relieved the tightened senses of the new men. It was as if he had hit his fingers with a tack hammer at home.

He held the wounded member carefully away from his side so that the blood would not drip on his trousers.

The captain of the company, tucking his sword under his arm, produced a handkerchief and began to bind with it the lieutenant's wound. And they disputed about how the binding should be done.

The lieutenant is more concerned with his trousers and the captain's bandaging technique than he seems to be with the fact that he was shot. Crane underscores this by comparing the lieutenant's behavior in a war setting to the way he would react to a mishap at home. Even the captain "tucks" his sword under his arm, since the delay is not so significant that he should sheath his meaningful weapon.

However, the next paragraph uses the words "madly," "agony," and "struggling," and in an instant, the battle pitches from mundane, comic, and trivial, to wrenching, ominous, and fatal. The flag "suddenly sank down as if dying," and Fleming sees "a sketch in gray and red dissolve" into men charging the regiment—the Rebel army. He hears "wild yells," but also jeers from the veteran regiments as they mock the fear and hesitation of the inexperienced soldiers. Fleming is seeing firsthand that war is contradictory, changing, confusing, and horrible. A man is crushed, and the blue regiment is "motionless, carven," and no one is clear on what is actually happening as the line retreats.

Amid the chaos, Fleming thinks only that now, if he were to see the "composite monster," he would flee.

Chapter 5 opens with a pause in the battle. Fleming recalls his home and the advent of a circus parade, but the dominant color is yellow, the same color as the corpse's uniform and the ignominious packet Wilson handed him prior to the battle. The houses he recalls as "sober," and the circus lady rides a "dingy" horse, and the band has a "faded" chariot. After the first thrilling and horrifying surge of battle, home has become a decaying idea for Fleming, and he experiences the soldier's conundrum: hatred of battle and war but the visceral appreciation of its incomparable intensity. From Crane to Hemingway to O'Brien, writers have described the difficulty of veterans to resolve their love of home with the boredom and aimlessness they experience there when compared to their memories of warfare. While readers never see Henry Fleming return from the battlefield (and some critics have suggested he never makes it), the beginning of this chapter suggests he has taken to the excitement of the battlefield, and that any homecoming he might have would result in difficulties.

Fleming has little time to muse on the idea. Conklin is knotting a red handkerchief about his neck as someone shouts "Here they come!" The swarm has gone from gray to brown, the color of turned earth, of the damaged, winter-scarred land referred to in the opening passage of the book. Brown is more elemental than gray, suggesting something more stalwart than the fog and smoke, more irresistible.

The officers holler for the soldiers to hold off the enemy, their manner scolding and "resentful." The soldiers are afraid. Fleming himself has sweat streaming down his face, "which was soiled like that of a weeping urchin," by which Crane reminds us again of the youthfulness of Henry Fleming. But then, as Fleming fires a wild shot,

> He suddenly lost concern for himself, and forgot to look at a menacing fate. He became not a man but a member. He felt that something of which he was a part— a regiment, an army, a cause, or a country—was in a crisis. He was welded into a common personality which was dominated by a single desire. For some moments he could not flee no more than a little finger can commit a revolution from a hand.

Lost in the battle, Fleming is only obliquely aware of his fellow soldiers. The enemy blurs. Just as he begins to feel fatigue, he enters

... a red rage. He developed the acute exasperation of a pestered animal, a well-meaning cow worried by dogs. He had a mad feeling against his rifle, which could only be used against one life at a time. He wished to rush forward and strangle with his fingers. He craved a power that would enable him to make a world-sweeping gesture and brush all back. His impotency appeared to him, and made his rage into that of a driven beast.

In essence, Fleming reverts to an animal state. Gone are the ideals of becalmed man brought to a gentle state by advances of society. Just as Fleming is here a "pestered animal," so, too, are the soldiers and the army itself frequently compared to animals. For this scene, Fleming's transition marks the first critical change of the book, the moment when he encounters war and is, psychologically, reduced to a more primal state. All of his ideas and views are challenged and, at least in the moment, he abandons them. His preconceptions and ideas about valor will come back and make trouble for him later, but at the critical battle in this chapter, Fleming's outlook has changed.

He notes how "there was a singular absence of heroic poses." The descriptions of the soldiers at that point focus on the jerking motions, on the din, on the contradictory elements of both machine and confusion that characterize their motions. The officers are not "picturesque," either. The lieutenant hollers at a fleeing soldier, other officers howl, men drop "here and there like bundles," the captain is killed. Crane describes the random carnage, splintered knee joints, grunts, hapless screaming.

And then the battle stops. Fleming looks around himself, sees twisted bodies, hears artillery still booming, and as wounded men pass, Fleming likens them to "a flow of blood from the torn body of the brigade." The dark lines of troops suggest thousands. When he sees the flags, the red dominates.

The youth is about to be proud of himself. He had survived. But the passage makes clear that his actions were not the result of decision or thought or valor, but of animalistic adrenaline, fear, and, perhaps, training. He had reacted only in ways that the situation allowed. His description revealed he felt boxed in, and his automatic fighting he had revealed as animalistic.

Thus, there is a grim and foreshadowing irony to the last paragraph. In it, he notes the blue of the sky, equating the color of the uniforms and the sky, equating the valor of the Union's cause and bearing with the grandeur of nature. Even though the two things are of different color, the use of the same undifferentiated primary term shows Crane conflating, in Fleming's mind, the two things. However, just as Fleming celebrates nature and the fact that it continued despite the savagery of the field, he is unaware of the dark side of his animalistic reactions that await in the future chapters, how fear will lead to a flight reaction rather than a fight reaction. He is also not yet thinking of the cruelty of nature's continuing despite the fighting. In this instance, the natural world remains beautiful, but that is only due to his interpretation of it. Fleming does not yet see that the natural world is uncaring.

In **chapter 6** the youth awakens and realizes, "So it was all over at last! The supreme trial had been passed. The red, formidable difficulties of war had been vanquished."

He is proud of himself, caught in an "ecstasy of self-satisfaction." He walks about the scene with warm greetings for the men he now perceives as his brothers-in-arms, but his basking in the glow of what he sees as a supreme accomplishment is short-lived. Fleming is about to learn a sobering truth, that life goes on. As does battle. And that wars are comprised of battles that lead one into the other. Just because the regiment fended off one assault does not mean there will be no further assaults. And sure enough, as the men take positions to fight the oncoming enemy again, Fleming is stunned, and the valor and strength he had felt is transformed. Note the use of color again, and the tone of the language as the battle starts again:

Surely, he thought, this impossible thing was not about to happen. He waited as if he expected the enemy to suddenly stop, apologize, and retire bowing. It was all a mistake.

But the firing began somewhere on the regimental line and ripped along in both directions. The level sheets of flame developed great clouds of smoke that tumbled and tossed in the mild wind near the ground for a moment, and then rolled through the ranks as through a grate. The clouds were tinged an earthlike yellow in the sun rays and in the shadow were a sorry blue. The flag was sometimes eaten and lost in this mass of vapor, but more often it projected, sun-touched, resplendent.

In the youth's eyes there came a look that one can see in the orbs of a jaded horse. His neck was quivering with nervous weakness and the muscles of his arms felt numb and bloodless. His hands, too, seemed large and awkward as if he was wearing invisible mittens. And there was a great uncertainty about his knee joints.

The passage contains several repeating aspects of Crane's style. The colors again point to how Crane wishes the reader to interpret the scene; the sickly yellow taints the clouds, and the blue—until now synonymous with the demonstrated virtue and strength of the Union line—is "sorry," reflecting the change in the line after the first exchange. Note, too, that the flag reflects the state of the troops; just as the troops vary in their response, and the line moves, so, too, does the flag. Earlier, as the troops had felt the "red rage" in battle, so, too, was the flag dominated by the red in its colors. The colors are specific, primary, vivid, comprising a scene that is bolder than it might actually have been, such that the flashes of color both reveal mood and compose a scene for which the impressions are of greater importance than the facts.

The scene also makes yet another animal comparison. Fleming's physical state is compared to an overworked and benumbed horse, the fatigue putting him at the edge of collapse. Crane's comparison underscores his theme regarding how men turn to their baser instincts in warfare, regardless of any high rhetoric or ideals.

The oncoming soldiers also awaken fear in Fleming. In the next paragraphs, he imagines the rebels to be a fighting force far beyond the regiment in skill. They become "an onslaught of redoubtable dragons." Fleming sees two otherwise brave-seeming men run, followed by others, and fear overtakes him and he runs as well. He speeds to the rear, dodges the lieutenant (who tries to stop him) and continues. Just as he fought in the last skirmish out of reflex and fear, he also runs out of similar instinct. He is described as running "blind," unaware of what he is doing, only "dimly" seeing others. He dodges artillery and shell explosions with their "livid lightning," and as he runs past a battery, begins to feel that he and the other runners are the only smart people. He regards the gunners as "altogether unaware of the impending annihilation." To the youth, all is lost, and he is smart to run. He thinks:

> The youth pitied them as he ran. Methodical idiot! Machine-like fools! The refined joy of planting shells in the midst of the other battery's formation would appear a little thing when the infantry came swooping out of the woods.

Fleming passes the rest of the artillery placements and, at last out of "the place of noises," he comes upon a general sitting on a horse. The general's only color is a "gleaming yellow," and he is reduced to looking "mouse-colored upon such a splendid charger." The humanity pales against the strength of the animal, and the "mind" behind the fighting is reduced to comparisons with a mouse, and a color heretofore identified with decay and sickness.

Fleming learns two things as he overhears the general. First, that the general hardly considers the troops individually; they are all part of larger machines, brigades and regiments, parts that inspire his irritation. Second, Fleming learns that the army has held the enemy. Annihilation did not occur. Crane puts off Fleming's reaction until the net chapter, but the general's reaction is all hubris, staring "upon the earth like a sun." Crane then uses a comparison to bring the general down a notch in the eyes of the reader. His celebrations are diminished: "he held a little carnival of joy on horseback." The general is a sad cartoon.

At the outset of **chapter 7** Fleming is mortified. He hears cheering from the "imbecile line," and a "yellow fog" moves in over the treetops, likely made from the smoke of the "clatter of musketry." The battle may be over for the moment, but now the line is advancing, moving into territory previously held by the Confederates.

Fleming has achieved some separation from the line, the battle, the war. In his previous confrontation, he had joined with the line, had become an automaton, had become subsumed by the action and the mechanical nature of fighting. Separated, compelled to rationalize his behavior, he tells himself he was "sagacious." He had lived to fight another day, given that annihilation was all but assured. But he grows "bitter" when he realizes he will have to face his comrades, all of whom he assumes remained behind (even though he ran with several others), and he expects "howls of derision." Lost in those thoughts, he continues to wander until he is deep into thick woods, far removed from battle:

Off was the rumble of death. It seemed now that nature had no ears.

This landscape gave him assurance. A fair field holding life. It was the religion of peace. It would die if its timid eyes were compelled to see blood. He conceived Nature to be a woman with a deep aversion to tragedy.

He threw a pine cone at a jovial squirrel, and he ran with chattering fear. High in a treetop he stopped, and, poking his head cautiously from behind a tree branch, looked down with an air of trepidation.

The youth felt triumphant at this exhibition. There was the law, he said. Nature had given him a sign. The squirrel, immediately upon recognizing danger, had taken to his legs without ado.

The laws of "nature," as Fleming sees it, supplant the laws of his mother's religion and of the men who form the army and its rules. Natural law has a "deep aversion" to tragedy. Fleming chooses to see only the representation given by a most bucolic setting, deep, untrammeled woods, ignoring the fact that the fields are nature, as are the violent rages and automatic fear responses that have governed much of his action to that point. Crane's psychological realism conflicts with and expands Fleming's version of natural law.

But it will get worse. As Fleming goes past a swamp and into deeper woods, he comes upon a place "where the high, arching boughs made a chapel." Within, "horror-stricken," he finds a corpse. The once blue uniform has decayed to green—a mix of blue and the yellow of decay. The eyes are gray, the hue of "a dead fish," and the mouth has gone from red to yellow. The skin, too, is gray. The colors here complete Crane's palette of decay and death. Fleming has found a rebuke to his musings deep in the chapel in nature: nature is as much ants feeding on necrotic flesh as it is bough-constructed chapels. He can no longer find comfort there. He flees.

In **chapter 8** Fleming runs from the deep woods and hears the sounds of battle again, a "crimson roar," and sees the "gray walls of vapor" where the battle is happening. Along the way, he has the realization that the battle he had fled was not the deciding conflict of the war. He realizes it was likely an insignificant skirmish in a battle that would barely register in the newspapers. Amid such sobering thoughts, he also feels his interest in seeing the war rekindle; "the battle was like the grinding of an immense and terrible machine to him. Its complexities and powers, its grim processes, fascinated him. He must go close and see it produce corpses." Then, he runs into a group of dead soldiers in a clearing. As he leaves them, he feels as though he has been an invader.

He soon encounters a line of wounded marching down a road away from the battlefield. The men are described and Crane makes matter-of-fact the gore and injuries. Fleming notices a man who has "the gray seal of death already upon his face," as well as a "tattered man, fouled with dust, blood and powder stain," who trudges near him for a while. Fleming does not yet realize that the "spectral soldier," the one gaping, still, and about to die, is Jim Conklin. Instead, he feels irritated by the "tattered soldier," the more so when the soldier asks where Fleming was "hit" in the battle. Fleming is too ashamed and embarrassed to answer, and is shaken by the question entirely.

Chapter 9 finds Fleming avoiding the tattered soldier. He looks at the wounded around him and envies them, wishing he had his own wound, "a red badge of courage." Thus we see that while Fleming has learned a lot about war, some of his romantic ideals are still in place. That said, his desire is not so much for the "courage" he sees in the wound, but for the sign of status that will save him from the derision of other soldiers on learning that he ran from battle. He wants some method to avoid shame.

However, as he thinks about it, the "spectral soldier" appears, like a "stalking reproach." He is walking but nearly dead, and the other wounded soldiers have gathered and are discussing him. Fleming notes his suffering, and tries to repel the other soldiers. Then he realizes the man is Jim Conklin. As Henry works to protect his friend, the other soldiers keep a distance. Conklin tells Fleming he was shot, and confesses his fear that he will fall and be run over by artillery wagons. Conklin maintains his kindness to Fleming even after it is clear he can do no more to help the boy, and Henry is deeply distressed.

As Henry is anguished, Jim begins to walk into the woods on his own, waving off the youth's offers of assistance. As Fleming watches Jim stalk into the woods, he soon follows, and realizes the tattered soldier has rejoined him, and is muttering behind him. Jim knows he will die, and is looking for a place away from the line so he might do it. Henry notes the "purpose" in Jim's face, and later, that the "tall soldier faced about as upon relentless pursuers." He entreats Henry to "Leave me be for a minnit."

When Conklin stops, his hands and face are bloody, and his side is wounded; his injuries parallel Christ's. The language continues with religious significance, echoing aspects of the Passion:

> They began to have thoughts of a solemn ceremony. There was something ritelike in these movements of the doomed soldier. And there was some resemblance in him to a devotee of a mad religion, blood-sucking, muscle-wrenching, bone-crushing. They were awed and afraid, They hung back lest he have at command a dreadful weapon.
>
> At last, they saw him stop and stand motionless. Hastening up, they perceived that his face wore an expression telling that he had at last found the place for which he had struggled. His spare figure was erect; his bloody hands were at his side. He was waiting with patience for something that he had come to meet. He was at the rendezvous. They paused and stood, expectant.

Jim's death is almost a dance, grotesque and fearsome. He writhes and Fleming looks on at the "ceremony." When Jim dies and falls to earth, the tattered soldier shouts, "God!" The utterance is perhaps a naming or a rebuke as well as an oath. When the flap of Jim's "blue jacket" opens, Fleming and the tattered soldier each see the wounds at his side; the wound and its terrible price is hidden by the blue display, by the uniform. The gaudy spectacle covers the cost of the fighting.

The chapter ends on a line that has attracted a great deal of attention, both for its impressionistic style and its hint at religious significance. Crane writes, "The red sun was pasted in the sky like a wafer." The sun's place is rendered temporary by the act of its being "pasted." At the same time, comparing the sun to a "wafer" at a moment of a redemptive death, at a death undergone to ease the suffering of others, at a place of "meeting," suggests a communion wafer. Finally, that Crane leaves the sentence on its own at the end of a pivotal chapter—indeed, the chapter from which the novel takes its title—underscores the significance of the line to the overall theme of the work.

Jim has died, and **chapter 10** opens with the tattered soldier talking again, reflecting with some awe on the strength and character of Jim Conklin. Aggrieved, Fleming finds the tattered soldier annoying, and wants to "screech out his grief."

They start walking, having resolved there was nothing they could do for Conklin. They are quiet for a while, until Henry realizes that it is very likely he will witness the death of the tattered soldier as well. The tattered soldier tries to reassure Fleming that he is not about to die, but as he does so, his conversation shortly afterward grows more nonsensical. As they walk, he regards Fleming and asks the youth how he was hurt. The questioning makes Fleming very uncomfortable, and then he grows angry: "He was enraged against the tattered man, and could have strangled him."

Instead, he abandons him. Fleming knows the tattered man will die, and he abandons him anyway, a crime he will later regret. As he does, he begins to envy the dead:

> He now thought that he wished he was dead. He believed that he envied those men whose bodies lay strewn over the grass of the fields and on the fallen leaves of the forest.
>
> The simple questions of the tattered man had been knife thrusts to him. They asserted a society that probes pitilessly at secrets until all is apparent. His late companion's chance persistency made him feel that he could not keep his crime concealed in his bosom. It was sure to be brought plain by one of those arrows which cloud the air and are constantly pricking, discovering, proclaiming those things which are willed to be forever hidden. He admitted that he could not defend himself against this agency. It was not within the power of vigilance.

Fleming is plagued with guilt and self-loathing, and is growing lost in the woods. His being lost mirrors his moral state as well; the indications of the battle, of nature, and his instinctive actions are at odds, and his psychological state is severely troubled. It changes how he views his surroundings and propels him to a worse state.

Chapter 11 opens as fear consumes Henry. The woods are filled with "brown clouds," the elemental earth reasserting itself. The line "wagons, teams, and men" also is swept along by fear, in clear retreat. The wagons become "fat sheep," docile animals figuring again in Crane's animal imagery. Henry is somewhat reassured at seeing the retreat, as it changes what he knows were cowardly actions into sane and sensible choices made by someone who knew what was coming.

By this point, it is clear Henry's yardstick for measuring his actions is the opinion of others, whereas the mature individual develops an internal measure of his or her deeds. Henry's maturation process is being foreshortened by the intensity of war, but is also complicated by the very rigid mythology of war and soldiering offered by the culture of the military, the press, and the popular ideas of Fleming's day. Crane's theme in the novel is not about moral reactions to the war; the ideas, goals, and merits of the Civil War in America are never addressed in the book and are entirely beside the point. Rather, Crane considers the difference between the private thoughts of individuals and their public actions. Henry Fleming reads as immature because he still believes his actions have a mutable morality, one determined by what others know of his "secrets" and his motives, and how his actions can appear.

As he begins to feel more hopeful about his state, the infantry appears. The men are grave, stern, and driven. They feel "the pride of their onward movement" when others are slow. Henry watches them pass, headed back into battle (and not to retreat, as he had surmised), and as he watches them pass:

> ... the black weight of his woe returned to him. He felt that he was regarding a procession of chosen beings. The separation was as great to him as if they had marched with

weapons of flame and banners of sunlight. He could never be like them. He could have wept in his longings.

Henry's other mark of immaturity, of course, is failing to realize that the men he admires so much may well have their own envies, may well assume him to be valorous, may well be guarding their own failings like frail secrets.

As he marvels at their strength, he begins to imagine himself a "blue desperate figure" rushing to the front and dying before a "crimson assault," all murky colors gone, all conflict either in righteous blue or wrathful and evil crimson, and he would be "calmly killed on a high place before the eyes of all. He thought of the magnificent pathos of his dead body." When he imagines others seeing him in this way, he exaggerates all significance, making a classic boastful assumption of the young. To put it colloquially, Henry fails to notice that the war engaging millions of men in a young nation is not *all about him*.

He loves the idea of such a valorous show. As he contemplates it, however, he realizes the difficulties facing even an attempt to do so: he is separated from his regiment, he has no weapon, and he is bone tired. He also discovers a number of ailments afflicting him. While he proceeds slowly, he imagines the army being defeated, and that defeat would allow for "roundabout vindication of himself," as his actions would have been the work not of a coward, but of a "seer." In a paroxysm of self-protection, he has gone from being ready to die for the army to hoping that they have suffered crushing defeat. Finally, as he imagines strolling back into camp, he sees his comrades joking about his cowardice, and he worries that he has already become a joke among them, a "slang phrase."

Fleming does not have long to wallow in self-pity. **Chapter 12** opens as retreating Union soldiers come "sweeping out of the woods," their courage gone; Henry notes that "the steel fibers had been washed from their hearts." Crane then pokes some fun at Fleming:

The youth was horrorstricken. He stared in agony and amazement. He forgot that he was engaged in combating the universe. He threw aside his mental pamphlets on the philosophy of the retreated and rules for the guidance of the damned.

While an odd editorial aside in a book otherwise free of such judgments, it is perhaps better understood as Henry's becoming caustic with himself in the face of what is happening. He grows suddenly sober and chastises his own reflective behavior given that he should probably be running along with the rest of them, if he wishes to have a hide left to contemplate. Either way, he is too stunned to move, until he begins to wonder what is happening. Scurrying around, he tries to grab a soldier to ask what is happening. The man, scared and frustrated, smacks Henry with the butt of his rifle, and Henry falls writhing to the ground. He is wounded.

At length he stands. Disoriented, he begins to move with the other soldiers. Here, the language turns more figurative as Henry's grip on his surroundings is loosened significantly by the injury to his head. The officers curse "like fishwives," the artillery "were assembling as if for a conference," and the distant guns "belched and howled like brass devils guarding a gate." The images are unexpected and discordant, reflecting Henry's mental state. At the same time, the colors come into the scene well, rendering their impressionistic qualities. The mist is blue, the sky red, smothered by a cloud, and the forest purple. In the context of Henry's stumblings, the colors do not quite match the meaning they have accrued to this point in the novel. The blue may not be the preening or righteous army, the purple may not be the darker blend of war and rectitude. The colors are changing, mirroring the way Fleming is changing. The blow dealt him will result in significant events later, and it will provide him his own nadir within the chapter.

Colors continue—the "purple darkness," the "blue and somber sky"—as Henry finds the road again, this time empty of soldiers. As he stumbles, he encounters his past in memory. Henry has thrice, to this point, gone back to his past in his memory, and each time has occurred at a critical juncture in his character development: as he waits for war, as he heads into battle, and now as he deals with his own cowardly and selfish decisions. A theme for Crane is maturity through one's encountering and dealing with one's past, and here Fleming recognizes how distant and untroubled his past was, how little he knew.

As he is about to fall, he hears a "cheery voice" at his shoulder. He is assisted then by a strange man who helps him, almost magically, back to the regiment. Only after the man leaves does Henry appreciate the kindness and realize that he had not seen the man's face.

Given the important presence of religion in the preceding chapters, and the mythological overtones of the war, one could argue that the strange man operates as a *deus ex machina*. However, a few biographers have pointed out that Crane's life offers an incident, which occurred during the writing of *Red Badge*, that mirrors the content of chapter 12. Once on a visit to his brother, William, Crane ran out of money such that he had to stop taking trains and actually walk the last several miles to his brother's home. He was so undernourished and underclothed that he was found wandering in the road by two rural personalities who came to his aid. They half-carried him the rest of the way, telling cheery stories the entire time, and leaving him at the house, departing before Crane could thank them or even talk to them.

In **chapter 13** Henry staggers back into camp after he is pointed there by the kind stranger. The sentry he encounters first is Wilson, formerly the loud soldier. Wilson rushes to Henry's aid and, seeing the wound on his head from the rifle swing, assumes he has been shot. From Henry's garbling, Wilson constructs a story of what he thinks happened, and Henry lets Wilson repeat the story to others until it is established as fact. Wilson turns Henry over to a corporal, who brings him to a fire and sets him down to relax.

Henry sits and sees ghostly images of what he only later realizes are sleeping soldiers. He is still woozy from fatigue and the injury, and the camp scene is taking on a surreal air. When he sees a soldier sleeping while sitting upright, embracing his sword, Fleming sees him as "the picture of an exhausted soldier after a feast of war." Again, the odd and lyric comparison underscores Henry's mental state.

Wilson comes to Henry's aid after his patrol is over. He tends to Henry's wounds with the "bustling ways of an amateur nurse." While Henry is grateful for the water and the care Wilson provides, he is also irritated and exhausted. Wilson brusquely makes Henry sleep. Significantly, when Henry lays and falls asleep—the story of his wounding intact, the fighting now in the past—his deeds are secret with him, and he is "like his comrades."

When Henry awakens in **chapter 14**, the ominous color gray is back and the sound of fighting is in the air, distant. It had been cold in the night, and a light frost had settled on the sleeping regiment. As Henry awakens, he mistakes the sleeping men for corpses, and is momentarily horrified until he realizes he is in camp, and others are moving. The reader learns his perception is back to being relatively normal.

Wilson comes to check on Fleming and is calm and careful, even though his inexperienced hands hurt Fleming a bit. He is sharp with his friend, but Wilson won't rise to the fight like he used to. He laughs it off. He watches Henry eat, looking out for him. Henry notices the difference in Wilson:

The youth took note of the remarkable change in his comrade since those days of camp life upon the river bank. He seemed no more to be continually regarding the proportions of his personal prowess. He was not furious at small words that pricked his conceits. He was no more a loud young soldier. There was about him now a fine reliance. He showed a quiet belief in his purposes and abilities. And this inward confidence evidently enabled him to be indifferent to little words of other men aimed at him.

In other words, Wilson had matured. He no longer overcompensates for perceived shortcomings, as Fleming will come to do in the following scenes. As Fleming has the realization, he tells Wilson, and the other soldier laughs it off, saying he was a "pretty big fool" in those days. They speculate on what will happen with the regiment, Henry tells Wilson of Conklin's death, and as they are talking an argument breaks out nearby. As Wilson tries to calm things down, the other soldiers get more angry but their zeal to fight subsides. Fleming comments again how Wilson has changed, as though he cannot yet really believe it. Finally, Wilson soberly tells Henry that the soldiers thought half the regiment was lost, but that men kept coming back, and Henry is restored to a degree of comfort: his story is now part of a larger story, and his deeds are protected.

Chapter 15 opens with the regiment waiting for the command to march. Here Henry realizes he still has Wilson's "yellow" package from the day before, and thus still holds over Wilson the embarrassing incident of the "lugubrious words." He starts to say something, then stops. Henry feels "immensely superior," revealing that despite what he has been through, his maturation is not yet complete. The flash of superiority helps him to rebuild his level of removal from a frank look at his thoughts and actions:

> He adopted toward him an air of patronizing good humor.
>
> His self-pride was now entirely restored. In the shade of its flourishing growth he stood with braced and self-confident legs, and since nothing could now be discovered he did not shrink from an encounter with the eyes of judges, and allowed no thoughts of his own to keep from an attitude of manfulness. He had performed his mistakes in the dark, so he was still a man.
>
> Indeed, when he remembered his fortunes of yesterday, and looked at them from a distance he began to see something fine there. He had license to be pompous and veteranlike.

Later in the chapter, though, as he imagines telling others of what battle is really like, he reveals that he has experienced some growth; he will dispel what he terms the "vague feminine formula for beloved ones doing brave deeds on the field of battle without risk of life." He knows enough to understand that war has a cost, but does not yet understand that his individual actions have moral consequence—whether or not anyone witnesses his deeds.

The chapter illustrates this when Wilson eventually works up the courage to ask Fleming for the packet of letters. Fleming gives Wilson the papers without comment, mostly because he can't think of a sufficiently "remarkable comment." He instantly forgets his original intention and instead is smugly satisfied with having come off as holding his tongue. "It was a generous thing," he thinks. Unlike Wilson, Fleming muses, he had never done anything so public that he had to be embarrassed for it. "He had never been compelled to blush in such a manner for his acts; he was an individual of extraordinary virtues." His attitude is patronizing and condescending to Wilson.

Further, he looks forward to more such condescension. Reflecting on his battle behavior, he realizes his "laurels" were insignificant. "Still," he reasons, imagining a rapt audience, "in a district where laurels were infrequent, they might shine."

Regaining strength and attitude, Fleming begins **chapter 16** marching with his regiment to relieve another command. The battle is more abstract there; the sounds are more muted, the images covered in fog. Flags are "idle," trees make "curtains," the lines of men become "dark bodies."

Waiting, Henry feels his oats. As the men mutter discontentedly about the officers and planning, Henry joins in, and is soon holding forth on the valor and dedication of the company. When a sarcastic soldier suggests "Mebbe yeh think yeh fit th' hull battle yestirday, Fleming," Henry is stung back to being quieter, discerning the other soldier as a "threat." Before long, though, Henry is back to complaining, this time about being marched around, being chased, and as he begins to get lathered about the subject, the lieutenant comes to the back and is "obliged to vent some of his inward dissatisfaction upon his men."

Afterward, the men await the approaching "tempest." Time moves slowly—an idea now a cliché, but that when Crane wrote it, was a new and expressive way of conveying the idea of fear. He also conveys the sensation of the forces compelling them to fight: "They stood as men tied to stakes."

In **chapter 17** another battle engages, and Crane's style amplifies again. Readers see the return of animal imagery, impressionistic use of color and metaphorical language, religious comparisons, and Fleming's pointed and tense consciousness.

The animal imagery highlights the change in the men as they face their "relentless foe." The other army "badgered" them, such that Fleming feels like a "kitten chased by boys." As Fleming crouches behind a tree to wait for a chance to attack, his "teeth set in a curlike snarl," while the enemy become "flies sucking insolently at his blood." In Fleming's imagination,

> ... the fighters resembled animals tossed for a death struggle into a dark pit. There was a sensation that he and his fellows, at bay, were pushing back, always pushing fierce onslaughts of creatures who were slippery. . . .
>
> The blue smoke-swallowed line curled and writhed like a snake stepped upon. It swung its ends to and fro in an agony of fear and rage.

The imagery of war regains its metaphorical brilliance as well. The rifle shots are "beams of crimson" and "knifelike fire." Fleming's rage becomes a "dark and stormy specter," a precise echo of the image that accompanied Jim Conklin's death. His thoughts of death lead him to thinking he "would have given his life for a revenge of seeing their faces in pitiful plights." He wishes to "smash into pulp the glittering smile of victory which he could feel upon the faces of his enemies."

The change in Fleming is mirrored in the change in language. The style in this chapter is far less reportorial than in the first encounter, and Fleming's thoughts are not of fear or of the high drama of romantic conquests and daring deeds. The imagery is violent, and his thoughts are only of hate, so much so that when he thinks he is shot, he is not sure, and does not check. "He did not think more on it."

Even amid the pain of smoke and fire, he keeps going, fueled by war rage, and when the enemy retreats a bit, he is actually disappointed, and reluctantly returns to his position. He misses that a lull has happened. At that point, having performed as a "barbarian" in front of his comrades, he realizes he has achieved the public show of valor, and he begins to reflect upon it. It is not, after all, as he had expected it be. Just as he had been surprised to learn that fear and reflex happen without much decision-making, he has just discovered that what passes for valor is often the same kind of reaction: instant, unknowing, instinctive.

As he thinks about it, the religious imagery of the chapter intensifies. While earlier Fleming had referred to the universe being against him, causing him to hate it, "the little gods and big gods," he feels, with the admiration of his fellow soldiers upon him, as a "war devil," who had fought "like a pagan who defends his religion." The pagan imagery is important; Fleming has passed from Christian gentility and gentleness to something that to him feels as powerful but very different in character. As if to underscore the transformation, the chapter ends with the forest having changed. In previous chapters, the forest had attained the status of a chapel. At the end of chapter 17, blood rites have changed it:

> The forest still bore its burden of clamor. From off under the trees came the rolling clatter of the musketry. Each distant thicket seemed a strange porcupine with quills of flame. A cloud of dark, as from smoldering ruins, went up toward the sun now bright and gay in the blue, enameled sky.

The sky, the province of the benevolent god that oversees nature, remains blue (ordered and ostentatious, just like the unbloodied army) and calm while underneath it, the church, in which nature is revered, burns.

The company pauses at the opening of **chapter 18**, and as the battle rages around them, they hear its noise. A wounded soldier is "thrashing about in the grass" as Fleming and Wilson decide to seek water. As they do, they spot a house, and a typically comforting domestic image is changed by their noticing "one window, glowing a deep murder red." The air is "always occupied by a blaring."

Amid the horror, Wilson and Fleming see a "jangling general" (comic in his finery) nearly ride his horse over a wounded man in the road. The general, seemingly oblivious to the man he nearly injures, passes, and is met by other officers. As the officers speak, Wilson and Fleming hear firsthand the regard in which they and others in their regiment are held by the officers. The troops are all referred to as numbers, and one officer refers to the 304th, Fleming's group, as fighting "like a lot 'a mule drivers."

After giving the order to send in the regiment, the general says, "in a sober voice, 'I don't believe any of your mule drivers will get back.'" As the other man rides away, the general smiles.

Fleming and Wilson are astonished. Their ideas about the generals are, to a degree, confirmed: the generals don't care, and their planning leaves something to be desired. But the other realization, and one that Fleming himself will feel quite powerfully, is how insignificant his own actions are, in stark contrast to the significance he himself had assigned to his fleeing and his valorous fighting display. All the glory and shame he had imagined are false in the face of knowing that few will ever note or care what he does. Fleming feels "he had been made aged. New eyes were given him."

In that way, external affirmation or glory are, to a degree, removed for Fleming as motivating factors. He had heard the officer speak of the regiment "as if he referred to a broom."

Fleming and Wilson return to the camp and tell what they heard. The other men react "with a hundred varieties of expression." As they prepare for battle and the oncoming order to charge, they settle into a grim acceptance of what is to come. As well, the arena in which they fight shrinks while the rest of the world grows large in their understanding. The futility of their experience, of courage or flight, is cast in high relief by the world's interest "in other matters":

> None of the men's faces were mirrors of large thoughts. The soldiers were bended and stooped like sprinters before a signal. Many pairs of glinting eyes peered from the grimy faces toward the curtains of the deeper woods. They seemed to be engaged in deep calculations of time and distance.
>
> They were surrounded by the noises of the monstrous altercation between the two armies. The world was fully interested in other matters. Apparently, the regiment had its small affair to itself.

As the charge is about to begin, Fleming considers the part of the exchange he and Wilson had kept to themselves, of how the officers knew a charge by the 304th was suicide. But Fleming also sees then, ironically, how the other men knew already what he could not bear to say. A man says, "We'll git swallowed." The secret was meaningless.

Chapter 19 opens as the charge begins as the line falls "slowly forward like a toppling wall." The charge begins on a resigned note, but as Fleming realizes the chase is on, he embodies it. He is again filled with murderous rage and, soiled and screaming, his "red and inflamed features surmounted by the dingy rag with its spot of blood," his red badge of courage, he looks "to be an insane soldier."

The red badge is described in chapter 17, and reappears in this opening description as well. While Fleming has acquired his "badge," it is ill-gotten and, were the story of its origin known, embarrassing. Now, however, the spot is given its proper significance; it is but a "spot." The wished-for thing is subsumed in the actual cost and bearing of war. The wound has become nothing, as nothing is known about it, and the behavior

Fleming exhibits is no more a choice than is his "insane" appearance. He is all adrenaline, reflex, and reaction. The "red badge" has become ironic.

Fleming runs through shells exploding in "crimson fury," past men "punched by bullets," and into a "clearer atmosphere." Once in the open, facing the enemy as defined by "gray walls and fringes of smoke," suddenly the impressionistic qualities of the landscape fix into specifics, in a passage that has attracted the attention of critics and the admiration of readers and writers, for it approximates the altered consciousness, the revelation of battle:

> It seemed to the youth that he saw everything. Each blade of the green grass was bold and clear. He thought that he was aware of every change in the thin, transparent vapor that floated idly in sheets. The brown or gray trunks of the trees showed each roughness of their surfaces. And the men of the regiment, with their starting eyes and sweating faces, running madly, or falling, as if thrown headlong, to queer, heaped-up corpses—all were comprehended. His mind took a mechanical but firm impression, so that afterward everything was pictured and explained to him, save why he himself was there.

In the moment of change, the battle becomes a series of its particulars, and not the impressionistic clutter of previous battles. At the same time, his dreams and visions and internal arguments and angst disappear. He is unsure what he is doing there. But, ironically, Fleming's dash to clarity inspires the soldiers, who launch into the "delirium that encounters despair and death, and is heedless and blind to the odds. It is a temporary but sublime absence of selfishness."

Fleming leaves himself, and in so doing, becomes the ideal of valor for the others.

As they run out of energy, and "become men again" at the end of the charge, they realize they have not gone far, and for all the glory and freedom of the moment, they are soon under "yellow" fire. By this point in the novel, the color should be clear indication that the fight will not go well. They stop, several are shot, and in an instant, the lieutenant is yelling at them to return, his features "black" with rage, indicating both the vileness and distance he embodies.

It is Wilson who next exemplifies valor. As the men head back, the lieutenant exhorting them the whole way, Wilson kneels to fire, and the men are rejuvenated. They begin to fire as well, and to advance on the enemy's position. Wilson's moment does not last long, but its inclusion shows how the two young soldiers are each moving toward maturity and each are committing actions—however reactive or involuntary—that result in public displays of valor honestly earned.

As the charge continues, Fleming moves to stay close to the flag. He has, to this point, noticed the flag in each battle, and followed it. The flag has operated as a metaphorical indicator of the life of the regiment, though it is clear Fleming understands it operating as a protector:

Within him, as he hurled himself forward, was born a love, a despairing fondness for this flag which was near him. It was a creation of beauty and invulnerability. It was a goddess, radiant, that bended its form with an imperious gesture to him. It was a woman, red and white, hating and loving, that called him with the voice of his hopes. Because no harm could come to it he endowed it with power. He kept near, as if it could be a saver of lives, and an imploring cry went from his mind.

In the mad scramble he was aware that the color sergeant flinched suddenly, as if struck by a bludgeon. He faltered, and then became motionless, save for his quivering knees.

He made a spring and a clutch at the pole.

In his zeal to save and have the flag, Fleming has to wrest the flag from the dying color guard. But once he has it in hand, the youth feels imbued with its properties.

In **chapter 20** Wilson and Fleming return with the flag to find disorder. Officers are screaming orders, telling the men to do "conflicting and impossible things." The mood of the men is grim. Fleming and Wilson tousle a bit over the flag, and Fleming actually pushes Wilson at one point so that he may keep the flag. The soldiers are stunned, having "accepted the pelting of the bullets with bowed and weary heads" with the understanding that it might do some good. Upon realizing "that they had attempted to conquer an unconquerable thing there seemed to arise a feeling that they had been betrayed." The officers had misused them, and they do not like it.

The lieutenant is shot, and his arm hangs uselessly. But he seems unmoved by it, just as he is unmoved by the plight of his soldiers, and highly displeased with their performance. However, when he tries to yell, he tries to gesture, and cannot, and swears. He is a picture of impotence.

Fleming, on the other hand, *feels* impotent but is actually a well of developing power. He is beginning to have genuine feeling for his comrades, and he is also developing the wrath he had seen in other experienced soldiers. The reader knows his maturation is not complete, however, as he has not yet attained the philosophical bearing of Conklin. But as he does now think of the others in his unit, he is getting closer to Conklin in aspect.

While he does feel that "the retreat of the mule drivers was a march of shame," he also knew:

> ... that he and his comrades had failed to do anything in successful ways that might bring the little pangs of a kind of remorse upon the officer ... the youth allowed the rage of the baffled to possess him. This cold officer upon a monument, who dropped epithets unconcernedly down, would be finer as a dead man, he thought. So grievous did he think it that he could never possess the secret right to taunt truly in answer.
>
> He had pictured the red letters of curious revenge. "We *are* mule drivers, are we?" And now he was compelled to throw them away.

He presently wrapped his heart in the cloak of his pride and kept the flag erect. He harangued his fellows, pushing against their chests with his free hand. To those he knew well he made frantic appeals, beseeching them by name. Between him and the lieutenant, scolding and near to losing his mind with rage, there was felt a subtle fellowship and equality. They supported each other in all manner of hoarse, howling protests.

As he feels affinity with the lieutenant, his pride is no longer puffed by fear. Rather, it is built on the foundation of his deeds and the deeds he has witnessed from the other soldiers. While the retreat was humiliating, he also understands that "the regiment was a machine run down." He realizes the other soldiers feared the return to the battle, and that "it was difficult to think of reputation when others were thinking of skins. Wounded men were left crying on this black journey." Then, the next skirmish commences.

Henry assumes "the attitude of the color bearer in the fight of the preceding day." Bullets are everywhere, and men are either shouting to fight or craven and running. The lieutenant, he notices, is calm, holding his sword "in the manner of a cane." The lieutenant is now down from the horse, among the men, and his stolid bearing is impressing Fleming. He doesn't speak until he sees the rebels charging, and then orders the regiment to fire, and they do. Fleming notices briefly that the uniforms on the rebels are new, before they are awash in smoke. The two groups exchange volleys "in the manner of a pair of boxers," and the regiment repulses the charge. Having faced a threat and prevailed, the spirits of the men return. Fleming has led them. And at the end of the battle, they are returned to their former state: "They were men."

In **chapter 21** the regiment is relieved. But as they approach the lines, the veteran companies begin to taunt them. Fleming and the lieutenant grow angry, and the men grow sullen. Then, as the soldiers turn to look back over the ground they had covered, Fleming realizes the reason for the taunts and is himself embarrassed. He discovers that "the distances, as compared with the brilliant measurings of his mind, were trivial and ridiculous." Once again, a great battle and noble actions are, on reflection, when adjusted for perspective, insignificant. Even comic.

As well, Henry lapses back into self-satisfaction. He reflects on his own performance and is pleased. But the contrast of his self-regard and the real achievements of the veterans is shown subtly in Crane's use of color in the segment. Before Henry takes a moment to recall his actions, the reader is given two lines describing the scene. Recall that colors like gold and silver tend to be reserved in the book for the highest actions and ideals, and that red is savage and animal, the bloated war god:

> It seemed, then, that there was bitter justice in the speeches of the gaunt and bronzed veterans. He veiled a glance of disdain at his fellows who strewed the ground, choking with dust, red from perspiration, misty-eyed, disheveled.

A general rides into the group and chastises the colonel, saying that the regiment was just a hundred feet short of a "pretty success," and that the "mud diggers" failed. When the general leaves, the colonel begins swearing, in a manner similar to the way the lieutenant used to swear, while the lieutenant himself firmly defends the fighting the men did. The other soldiers grumble, and then Fleming delivers a Conklin-esque statement:

> The youth developed a tranquil philosophy for these moments of irritation. "Oh well," he rejoined, "he probably didn't see nothing of it at all and got mad as blazes, and concluded we were a lot of sheep, just because we didn't do what he wanted done. It's a pity old Grandpa Henderson got killed yesterday—he'd have known that we did our best and fought good. It's just our awful luck, that's what."

Fleming has let the men know his own thoughts, turning private consolation into a public act. He is a leader, and is maturing. While he has reflected on his role in battle, he has not dwelt on it after the latest encounter in the ways he had previously. The only thing remaining to happen to complete his understanding of courage and valor is for his decisive actions (rather than his mere reactions) to bear some reaction, and for him to know of some affirmation. Thus is the case, when soldiers appear, telling of how the lieutenant had met the colonel and the latter had praised both Wilson and Fleming. Fleming, in particular, is praised for carrying the flag—a valorous action that he had actually *chosen* to do.

Battle recommences in **chapter 22**. Fleming is again a witness of fantastical and fragmented images, but instead of cowering or raging, he stands, "erect and tranquil" with "serene self-confidence." He holds the standard, and as such, becomes the standard. He is able to see and understand all the movements, and he captures dozens of images, part of the battle but divorced from sequence, strobing before him. Color is again important, in the "red discharges" of the guns and their "crimson flare," the battle flags fly "like crimson foam" such that he cannot tell which side is winning, and the lines of men are "dark-blue," as if their resolve is bristling in the color of their uniforms. Where the regiment fights is a "smoke-wall penetrated by the flashing points of yellow and red."

When there is a pause, it is "churchlike," bringing again to the fore the religious overtones of the battle experience and the metaphor of Henry Fleming's "baptism" in the rites of the war god. The psychic distance between Henry and the actions of his regiment is underscored when, soiled and "resmudged," the men become "swaying bodies, black faces, and glowing eyes." The flag hangs silently over Fleming, "so absorbed was he," as he had become "absorbed as a spectator."

He sees the enemy descend upon the regiment and, despite the "plumping volley" the regiment fire in defense, the rebels begin "briskly to slice up the blue men." As they brace for a "great struggle," Crane cues the reader to the significance of their actions with the description of "white clinched teeth" that shine out of the fray. Fleming is angered as he sees their effort and recalls the scorn of the general who called them mud diggers. He cannot move he is so embittered.

Then, he begins to see the injured: "The regiment bled extravagantly." Crane describes a man shot through the cheeks, in full grisly detail. Other bodies are "twisted into impossible shapes." Fleming sees the weary lieutenant and Wilson, and notes that "the fire of the regiment had begun to wane and drip." He can no longer simply act as witness. His maturation requires that he take what he knows and act.

At the beginning of **chapter 23**, Henry Fleming knows they must charge, and he looks at the men, their weariness and their filth and injuries, and knows it will be difficult. But as they assent to the charge and steel themselves for it, Fleming notes that "It was a blind and despairing rush by a collection of men in dusty and tattered blue, over a green sward and under a sapphire sky, toward a fence, dimly outlined in smoke, from behind which spluttered the fierce rifles of enemies." While they are dirty, they are still "blue," they are still, in the code of the colors, *right*. Nature continues its unfeeling existence, placid and uncaring both above and below. Across the field is the vague unknown. Fleming has learned much about the conundrum in which the regiment is placed, and so it is fitting that he shifts to lead it. He is a veteran, a soldier, a man.

He begins to run, keeping the colors to the front. He has a "wild battle madness," and he wishes to deliver a "thunderous, crushing blow" to the enemy. As he gets closer, though, it is clear the enemy will retreat. They cannot stand up to what is now a "blue wave," and no longer merely a blue line.

A small group of resisters clusters around the enemy flag. The valor is again evident in that Crane employs the color white, this time for the eyes of the Union soldiers. And Fleming wants the flag; "its possession would be a high pride." However, as the soldiers clash, it is Wilson who tears the flag from the wounded Confederate soldier. Fleming congratulates his friend, and is happy for him. He does not, as he did some pages before, shove him roughly. Fleming has grown so that he can appreciate the success of others, even if it means his own goals go unfulfilled in the moment.

The chapter also marks the only time the enemy is described as men. In the early chapters, a few Confederate soldiers are referred to with specificity, but none with any description or humanity as they are described in chapter 23, as prisoners.

At the opening of **chapter 24** the battlefield grows quiet, and soon no muskets are heard, only the "stentorian speeches of the artillery" continue in the distance. Troops move on and prepare to march to the next battle. The soldiers have no way of knowing it, but Gettysburg is still around the corner, the horrors of which will dwarf what happened at Chancellorsville.

Fleming wonders, "Well, what now, I wonder?" His question can be read on several levels: he could be asking what is to come in the war, in his own development, in his understanding, with him and Wilson, and so on. It is a poignant question because of the experiences he has endured. It is also a question that has spurred some debate among literary critics trying to interpret the message at the end of the novel.

While he and Wilson both agree that "it's all over," Henry Fleming knows it's not, knows that "his mind was undergoing a subtle change." He has the urge to make sense of the extremities of what has happened, and so knows that, at the very least, thinking will continue to progress. From the comfortable distance of reflection, he is at first pleased: "Those performances which had been witnessed by his fellows marched now in wide purple and gold." They have about them the noblest colors of the book, the purple's mix of red war and blue righteousness, and gold's rarity and greatness.

However, they are only the known deeds. Here Henry must struggle within himself to reconcile his public deeds with what he privately knows:

A specter of reproach came to him. There loomed the dogging memory of the tattered soldier—he who, gored by bullets and faint for blood, had fretted concerning an imagined wound in another; he who had loaned his last bit of strength and intellect for the tall soldier; he who, blind with weariness and pain, had been deserted in the field....

... this vision of cruelty brooded over him. It clung near him always and darkened his view of these deeds in purple and gold. Whichever way his thoughts turned they were followed by the somber phantom of the desertion in the fields.

Henry is no longer worried about the understandable flight from combat; he is now bothered by his moral failing. It is that "cruelty" with which he must now grapple. As he hears the men around him discussing the battle, he comes to an understanding in his mind, a way to put his deeds—both noble and not—into perspective:

... gradually he mustered the force to put the sin at a distance. And at last his eyes seemed to open to some new ways. He found that he could look back upon the brass and bombast of his earlier gospels and see them truly. He was gleeful when he discovered that he now despised them.

With this conviction came a store of assurance. He felt a quiet manhood, nonassertive but of sturdy and strong blood. He knew that he would no more quail before his guides wherever they should point. He had been to touch the great death, and found that, after all, it was but the great death. He was a man.

So it came to pass that as he trudged from the place of blood and wrath his soul changed.

He is confident that, because his understanding has changed, he will not make the same mistakes again. However, many scholars point out that his "lover's thirst" for "images of tranquil skies, fresh meadows, cool brooks" reveals how naïve he remains, and how little he has learned of nature's indifference. As well, because the last line of the book has a golden ray among hosts of "leaden" rain clouds, it is unclear whether Fleming is even through fighting, much less that he will ever make it out of the war alive.

Of certainty is only that he has endured the war and that he has changed because of it. He has achieved manhood due to an internal struggle, fought against the backdrop of an epic struggle of men and nature. He has changed within the confines of the story, and so Crane's themes and observations about the psychology of struggle and redemption work and continue to resonate a century after it was written, and a century and a half after the episode it ostensibly illustrates.

LEE CLARK MITCHELL ON CRANE'S FORM AND STYLE IN THE NOVEL

Before turning to the larger questions raised by this elusive novel, we need to define the context in which any discussion must take place. Least obviously and most certainly, the battle fought by Henry Fleming's New York regiment occurred on May 1 and 2, 1863, at Chancellorsville, Virginia. Both this particular battle and the fact that it remains unnamed throughout shape the terms of a novel that offers impressions from the point of view of a combatant. After all, few soldiers during combat think of the names of places by which history labels their efforts, or in this case realized that a later generation would define the whole as the "Civil War" (indeed, the South continues to refer to the conflict as "The War Between the States"). Naming neither battle nor war, therefore, lends a more realistic effect to the novel precisely in the absence of local specification of what otherwise is so carefully described.

Crane's selection of Chancellorsville may have owed something to the influence of his brother, who was a Civil War buff and an expert on that particular battle. Stephen could not have helped consulting Edmund during the summer he spent writing at his brother's home. But the more compelling thematic reason is that the battle so perfectly represented the dark ironies of war. Twenty-seven thousand men died in a conflict whose immediate consequences seemed nil at best and at worst senseless; the North lost despite a decided superiority, the South won a merely Pyrrhic victory, and after two days both sides were left almost exactly where they had been. From military history, Crane could hardly have chosen a more futile episode, and his novel is scrupulously accurate in detailing the movements of troops and their engagements, the weather and general geography, even the specific local terrain of hills, rivers, and marshes.

The absence of labels and dates makes the narrative more, not less, effective by shifting attention away from either historical patterns or local meanings. Instead, the novel concentrates on the emotional violence of actual battle—any battle on any ground, between two armies in any war. Compounding this narrative effect throughout is the characters' lack of names; such epithets as "the loud soldier" and "the tattered soldier" serve to dramatize the irrelevance of social categories and the arbitrariness of linguistic convention. Crane's unwillingness to attach customary labels to individuals, places, or events illuminates by contrast how much can be lost when traditional identifications *are* made, when labels *are* used to order and yet to constrain experience.

Similarly, the novel breaks down grammatical order in the illogical transitions between image and subject, the fragmented syntax that contributes to Crane's characteristically abrupt or "nervous" style. The concentration on simple sentences at the expense of complex and compound constructions evokes a world lacking interdependency, one that refuses to hang together in predictable patterns. The heavily adverbial, prepositional prose rarely defines causal connections, instead compelling from the reader interpretations to fit the welter of images. Indeed, Crane reestablishes through stylistic means the primacy of sensory experience and implicates the reader in undifferentiated emotions through repetition and a stripping of diction. The very opening paragraph brings the narrative world alive, as the awakening army is imbued with an animistic sense. And thereafter, language refuses to insulate the reader by domesticating into familiar patterns the urgency of experience it represents.

Once alerted to the importance of its setting and having noted the implications of its wrenching style, we cannot fail to see the significance of the novel's strikingly dual structure. Nearly everything is repeated with formal precision, as two days of battle appear in twenty-five chapters that divide near the middle at Chapter 13/12, when Henry Fleming receives the "red badge" of an accidental head wound. The first twelve chapters expose his seeming cowardice, and his apparent heroism emerges in the last dozen. In turn, both halves of the novel divide, as the enemy charges twice in the opening half and on the second occasion panics Henry into flight; the motion is reversed in the last twelve chapters, when his own regiment charges twice and finally frightens the enemy into flight. Not to belabor a description of multiple other doublings and repetitions, the question they raise remains unchanged and central to the novel's interpretation. Such narrative mirroring can potentially show possibilities for an individual's growth and maturity, clarifying the development of certain traits by keeping the contexts the same. Alternatively, from an ironic perspective, such doubling can as easily expose the absence of genuine growth and dramatize how fully all stays unchanged despite superficially quite different results.

Either interpretation, in any event, must confront what John Berryman called Crane's "refusal to guarantee."[16] Whether at the specific level of diction or in larger terms of narrative endings, he leaves things inconclusive. As well, by subtly disrupting literary conventions, he presents an analogue for his readers of the very experience his characters face. Just as Henry Fleming cannot help interpreting his own ambiguous impulses, so the reader arrives at a novelistic "meaning" in the automatic process of deciphering Crane's grammar. That the reader's conclusions, like Henry's, depend on essentially conventional expectations reveals no more than that all interpretations are imposed upon chaotic experience and unruly texts. This has not, of course, always been clear to those offering to interpret the novel, which makes the history of its readings instructive for those coming to it afresh. Among his early admirers, for instance, both Edward Garnett and Joseph Conrad first recognized Crane as a literary "impressionist"—or as Conrad asserted: "*the only* impressionist and *only* an impressionist."[17] Neither one pursued this painterly analogy, and not until half a century later would the formalist New Critics probe its implications by examining the use in *Red Badge* of color imagery and synesthetic conceits. By revealing the novel's poetic complexities through a variety of close textual analyses, they exposed, sometimes inadvertently, its severe ambiguities.

A few critics have explored the novel in terms of Christian allegory, basing their readings on the suggestive initials and dramatic death of Jim Conklin and, in particular, on the concluding sentence of Chapter 9: "The sun was pasted in the sky like a fierce wafer." Accepting war as a process that contributes to man's final redemption, these interpreters have followed Robert W. Stallman's lead in reading the novel as a modern wasteland through which Henry Fleming wanders as a kind of Everyman. Freudians, on the other hand, have cleared the trail John Berryman first blazed by viewing the novel in largely Oedipal terms. Henry's outrage at a pattern of senseless violence is construed as a narrative enactment of Crane's own belated resistance to his parents' Methodist pieties and of the sense of betrayal he supposedly felt at his father's early death. Still others have read Crane in a literary-historical context that emphasizes his stature as a naturalist, comparing *Red Badge* with his other works as well as with the fiction of contemporaries like Theodore Dreiser, Frank Norris, and Jack London. In a universe where ineluctable forces control the individual, Henry Fleming becomes merely the victim of impulse and event, unable to enact a will that might break through fundamentally determinist patterns. Structuralists have more recently examined the verbal patterns of the novel to reveal the degree to which Henry arbitrarily projects a conventional moral-linguistic code onto the chaos of experience. His failure becomes one of interpretation, not action, and consists of his inability to recognize the reality he suffers as a verbal contrivance he himself has helped to make.

Notes

16. Berryman, *Stephen Crane*, pp. 287–8.
17. Stallman and Gilkes, ed., pp. 154–5

Kevin J. Hayes on Henry Fleming's Idealistic Visions

After surviving his first skirmish, Henry experiences tremendous relief. As a result, he no longer feels the need to envision how he will react in battle because he now concludes that he does indeed have the courage to face conflict. Self-satisfied, he can perceive himself from an external point of view and picture himself as a combat soldier: 'Standing as if apart from himself, he viewed that last scene. He perceived that the man who had fought thus was magnificent' (*RB* 30). His brief personal experience allows him to do something that his third-hand information gathering had not, to envision war as a participant and not merely as a spectator.

The pictures Henry can now see in his mind's eye are more recollections of recent events than projections of the future, however. They do not prepare him for further combat. Having mistaken the initial skirmish for the entire battle, he is unprepared for the following action. After assuming he has survived the battle without losing his nerve, he must now confront additional dangers. Neither his experience nor his imagination has prepared him for the new challenge. He loses courage and flees. After reaching a safe distance, however, he turns to witness the action he has fled: 'Then he began to run in the direction of the battle. He saw that it was an ironical thing for him to be running thus toward that which he had been at such pains to avoid. But he said, in substance, to himself that if the earth and the moon were about to clash, many persons would doubtless plan to get upon roofs to witness the collision' (*RB* 38). Those who have studied the prehistory of the cinema have identified the *badaud* or gawker as the nineteenth-century precursor of the cinema spectator, and this is the role Henry assumes upon fleeing the battle, as Crane's diction makes clear: 'He stood, regardant, for a moment. His eyes had an awe-struck expression. He gawked in the direction of the fight' (*RB* 39).

Henry continues to gawk as he wanders aimlessly behind the lines. His gawking does have a vague purpose, however: he seeks a way to reintegrate himself within the battle. Witnessing a line of wounded soldiers, Henry perceives them with a pang of envy: 'He conceived persons with torn bodies to be peculiarly happy. He wished that he, too, had a wound, a little red badge of courage' (*RB* 42). Callously, Henry perceives battle wounds not in terms of pain inflicted but in terms of symbolic value. Not even the sight of his mortally wounded friend Jim Conklin, whose side 'looked as if it had been chewed by wolves' (*RB* 45), dissuades Henry from his fascination with the emblematic value of battle scars.

The visible wound, an emblem of war rather than war itself, provides the key for Henry to imagine himself in battle. Understanding the results of battle abstractly, he can envision himself within the conflict:

> Swift pictures of himself, apart, yet in himself, came to him—a blue desperate figure leading lurid charges with one knee forward and a broken blade high—a blue, determined figure standing before a crimson and steel assault, getting calmly killed on a high place before the eyes of all. He thought of the magnificent pathos of his dead body.... He thought that he was about to start fleetly for the front. Indeed, he saw a picture of himself, dust-stained, haggard, panting, flying to the front at the proper moment to seize and throttle the dark, leering witch of calamity. (*RB* 51)

Seeing himself as a brave soldier, Henry creates an ideal image analogous to the emblems that so capture his attention. Like the emblems of war, Henry's pictures of himself are idealized abstractions. These personal images as a brave soldier become so obvious to him that, much like the cinema, they appear as moving pictures projected before a vast audience: 'He saw himself chasing a thought-phantom across the sky before the assembled eyes of mankind' (*RB* 56).

Though recovering the ability to envision himself in battle, Henry is still not ready to return to combat. Encountering a group of soldiers scattering from the front lines, he seeks answers to explain the confusion. He becomes so desperate for information that he clutches one of the soldiers and refuses to let go. Struggling to free himself, the other soldier swings his rifle, which hits Henry in the head with sufficient force to break the skin and cause some bleeding. Reuniting with his regiment late that evening, Henry tells a different story to explain the cause of his wound: 'I got shot' (*RB* 62). With these three words, Henry creates a narrative fiction to explain the cause of his wound and, in so doing, transforms an injury borne of confusion and panic into a red, yet surreptitious badge of courage.

As members of his regiment accept Henry's fiction as truth, he becomes quite self-satisfied, and his imagination lets him project himself as a hero to an audience of eager onlookers. He imagines himself 'in a room of warm tints telling tales to listeners' and foresees 'his gaping audience picturing him as the central figure in blazing scenes' (*RB* 73). Henry has transformed himself from a gawker to the object of gawkers. His wound lends credence to his lie, and Henry, now reunited with his unit, has successfully obscured his cowardly desertion.

Henry's behaviour beyond this point in the novel has been open to much critical debate. The controversy that has dogged *The Red Badge of Courage* over the course of its history involves the issue of Henry Fleming's maturity. Does Henry mature over the course of the novel, turning himself from frightened youth into courageous soldier? Or does he remain immature and self-centred even as he seems to enter combat? While the version of *Red Badge* edited by Henry Binder from Crane's original manuscript in the 1970s would seem to have answered the question once and for all, the controversy rages nonetheless.

Instead of asking whether Henry matures in battle, perhaps it would be more productive to ask how he copes with the dangers of battle. No longer fleeing from combat in a physical sense, Henry copes with danger through flights of fancy: he faces combat by enacting personal fantasies of bravery. Having formed mental images of battle, he now projects himself into those images.

The emblems of battle provide the connection between the real war and the combat Henry imagined. The flag becomes something he can cling to for its emblematic value. As Kermit Vanderbilt and Daniel Weiss have observed, the flag is Henry's fantasized charm against danger, and he endows it with extraordinary power.[4] Articulating what the flag means to Henry, Crane observes, 'It was a creation of beauty and invulnerability. It was a goddess, radiant, that bended its form with an imperious gesture to him. It was a woman, red and white, hating and loving, that called him with the voice of his hopes. Because no harm could come to it, he endowed it with power. He kept near as if it could be a saver of lives and an imploring cry went from his mind' (*RB* 88).

The flag has such power that it can animate the dead. Seeing the colour sergeant perish, Henry and a fellow soldier grab the flagstaff simultaneously: 'He made a spring and a clutch at the pole. At the same instant, his friend grabbed it from the other side. They jerked at it, stout and furious, but the colour-sergeant was dead and the corpse would not relinquish its trust. For a moment, there was a grim encounter. The dead man, swinging with bended back seemed to be obstinately tugging, in ludicrous and awful ways for the possession of the flag' (*RB* 88). Their struggle more closely resembles a boys' game than it does proper behaviour in battle. Henry finally captures the flag for himself by pushing his friend away.

The flag, combined with his surreptitious wound, combine to make Henry seem a ferocious soldier. Both flag and wound, after all, serve the same function in his mind. Both are emblems of war. Even as his emblems allow him to re-enter battle, Henry remains a spectator, however. Crane wrote, 'The youth, still the bearer of the colours, did not feel his idleness. He was deeply absorbed as a spectator. The crash and swing of the great drama made him lean forward—intent eyed, his face working in small contortions. Sometimes, he prattled, words coming unconsciously from him in grotesque exclamations. He did not know that he breathed; that the flag hung silently over him, so absorbed was he' (*RB* 99). Henry gawks in much the same way he had after running from battle. The difference is that, equipped with his emblems—red badge and red, white, and blue—he can imaginatively and actually project himself into battle.

Henry's seeming deeds of bravery become, for him, mental pictures to be viewed again and again:

> But the youth, regarding his procession of memory, felt gleeful and unregretting, for, in it, his public deeds were paraded in great and shining prominence. Those performances which had been witnessed by his fellows marched now in wide purple and gold, hiding various deflections. They went gaily, with music. It was pleasure to watch these things. He spent delightful minutes viewing the gilded images of memory. (*RB* 106)

What remains in his memory are not images of dead and dying, but images of himself. Henry has become the star of his own movie.

Note
4. Kermit Vanderbilt and Daniel Weiss, 'From Rifleman to Flagbearer: Henry Fleming's Separate Peace in *The Red Badge of Courage*', *Modern Fiction Studies*, 11 (Winter 1965/66), 378.

ALFRED KAZIN ON CONTRADICTIONS IN CRANE'S AUTHORIAL VISION

Out of this welter of enthusiasms that gave so many different clues to the future, there now emerged at the end of the century the one creative artist who sounded the possibilities open to his generation, though he fulfilled so few of them himself. In his day Stephen Crane stood as ... the fever-ridden, rigidly intense type of genius that dies young, unhappy, and the prey of lady biographers. Everything that he wrote in his twenty-nine years seemed without precedent.... But no conventional background or stimulus explains Crane's disposition to naturalism; neither the depression of the nineties, which never troubled him, nor the classic texts of European naturalism, by which he was generally bored. He was a naturalist by birth, so to speak; but there is nothing in the placid Jersey parsonage of the Reverend Jonathan Crane that explains the grim finality of mind, in its way an astounding capacity for tragedy, that devoured his fourteenth child. Sentimental critics have charged that Crane had a secret disaffection born out of his father's martyrdom in the service of Methodism and its apparent futility in the face of world events, but the surest thing one can say about Crane is that he cared not a jot which way the world went. No one was ever less the reforming mind; revolutions were something foreigners attempted that Hearst would pay good money to report. He accepted the world always, hating it always, plotting his way through it alone with a contempt that was close to pain.

Thomas Beer, who understood him best, hit at the secret of Crane's career when he wrote of a ruthless literary courage possible only to those who are afraid. Life tossed him up and down like a cork. To his last days he was tormented by disease and insecurity, greedy friends and witnesses of his genius who thought him a strangely convivial freak, stupid editors and pristine reviewers, the doltish open mouth of the public, pointing, giggling, and retailing stories. Crane never had a juvenile period, a time of test and error, of sentimental amplitude and human indirection. The hard, fixed boundaries which hold his books were iron clamps which were set early. All through that miserably unhappy life, even in the first days of glory when *The Red Badge of Courage* fell out of the heavens, he was the stricken boy Conrad saw at the end in Brede Place in England, sitting in a baronial pile eating his heart out in hack work, devoured by sycophants, always in some portentous torment, with the suffering eyes and the absurd mustache that fell over his face like the mask of old age.

The world was a ship, he wrote in one of his poems, that God had fashioned and let slip.

God fashioned the ship of the world carefully.
With the infinite skill of an All-Master
Made He the hull and the sails,
Held He the rudder
Ready for adjustment.
Erect stood He, scanning his work proudly.
Then—at fateful time—a wrong called,
And God turned, heeding.
Lo, the ship, at this opportunity, slipped slyly,
. . . .
Making quaint progress,
Turning as with serious purpose
Before stupid winds.
And there were many in the sky
Who laughed at this thing.

And no more than God could he hope to reclaim it. "I cannot be shown," he said once, "that God bends on us any definable stare, like a sergeant at muster, and his laughter would be bully to hear out in nothingness." He would not appeal against wrong, and he thought it monstrous to complain. Essentially uneducated, his resources lay in his physical senses, which he exploited with an intensity disproportionate to his strength and yet unequal to the fervor of his spirit. He read very little, and nothing surprised him more than when people who read his work condescendingly discovered his debt to Zola or to Tolstoy. *War and Peace*, which he knew, stimulated him to the boyish cockiness that flared at rare instances and was one of his more charming traits. "Tolstoy could have done the whole business in one-third of the time and made it just as wonderful," he laughed. "It goes on and on like Texas." He thought of writing a book entitled *Peace and War*, which would do "the job" better and be an answer to Tolstoy. It was perhaps because he had read so little, as Willa Cather suggested, that he felt no responsibility to be accurate or painstaking in his transcription of common events. Like every sensuous artist, he was a magnificent guesser, and nothing proved how deeply he had imagined the psychology of battle in *The Red Badge of*

Courage than his experience as correspondent in the Greco-Turkish War. "*The Red Badge* is all right," he said when he came out of it.

Yet the stark greatness of the novel did grow in part out of his instinctively intimate knowledge of American manners and character. As Carl Van Doren observed, the verisimilitude of the book testified to Crane's knowledge of the popular memory and authentic legends of the war. One side of him was the local village boy who never quite lost his feeling for the small talk and the casual pleasures of the American town, and it showed not only in the campfire talk of the men in *The Red Badge*, but in the charming little-boy stories in *Whilomville Stories* and the extraordinary transcriptions of Negro speech in *The Monster*. What kept Crane alive, in one sense, was just that feeling; without it his despair might have seemed intolerable and, for an artist of his sensibility, incommunicable. He baited the universe but never those village citizens who are as benign in his work as small-town fathers in the *Saturday Evening Post*. They were his one medium of fraternity, and his strong, quiet affection for them testifies to the unconscious strength of his personal citizenship.

A Tale of Everyman

In this sense even the most astonishing effects in *The Red Badge of Courage* reflect Crane's background, for its soldier-hero might have been any American boy suddenly removed from the farm to fight in a war of whose issues he knew little and in which his predominating emotion was one of consummate perplexity and boredom. As a novelist of war Crane anticipated the war studies of the future.... Crane's hero is Everyman, the symbol made flesh upon which war plays its havoc; and it is the deliberation of that intention which explains why the novel is so extraordinarily lacking, as H.L. Mencken put it, in small talk. Scene follows scene in an accelerating rhythm of excitement, the hero becomes the ubiquitous man to whom, as Wyndham Lewis once wrote of the Hemingway hero, things happen. With that cold, stricken fury that was so characteristic of Crane—all through the self-conscious deliberation of his work one can almost hear his nerves quiver—he impaled his hero on the ultimate issue, the ultimate pain and humiliation of war, where the whole universe, leering through the blindness and smoke of battle, became the incarnation of pure agony. The foreground was a series of commonplaces; the background was cosmological. Crane had driven so quickly through to the central problem that everything else seemed accessory in its effect, but he was forced to describe emotions in terms of color because the pressure behind so wholly concentrated a force drove him to seek unexpected and more plastic sources of imagery. Often he revealed himself to be a very deliberate tone-painter, as calculating and even mechanical a worker in the magnificent as Oscar Wilde or Richard Strauss. He aimed at picture qualities and he synthesized them so neatly that, like the movement of the hunters and the hunted in a tapestry of the medieval chase, they illustrated a world whose darkness was immensity. "In the Eastern sky there was a yellow patch, like a rug laid for the feet of the coming sun; and against it, black and pattern-like, loomed the gigantic figure of the colonel on a gigantic horse."

A Weariness of Life

Yet for all its beauty, Crane's best work was curiously thin and, in one sense, even corrupt. His desperation exhausted him too quickly; his unique sense of tragedy was a monotone. No one in America had written like him before; but though his books precipitately gave the whole esthetic movement of the nineties a sudden direction and a fresher impulse, he could contribute no more than the intensity of his spirit. Half of him was a consummate workman; the other half was not a writer at all. In his ambitious stories of New York tenement life, *Maggie* and *George's Mother*, the violence seemed almost celestial, but it was only Crane's own, and verbal; both stories suffer from excessive hardness and that strangely clumsy diction that Crane never learned to polish. In a great show piece like *The Open Boat* (drawn from an almost direct report of experiences in the Caribbean in the days when he was reporting the Cuban insurrection for New York newspapers) he proved himself the first great pyrotechnician of the contemporary novel; but the few superb stories are weighed down by hack work. The man who wrote *The Blue Hotel* also wrote more trash than any other serious novelist of his time. Even in buffooneries like his unfinished last novel, *The O'Ruddy*, there is the sense of a wasted talent flowing over the silly improvisation in silent derision. He had begun by astonishing the contemporary mind into an acceptance of new forms; he ended by parodying Richard Harding Davis in *Active Service* and [Robert Louis] Stevenson in *The O'Ruddy*. Yet it was not frustration that wore him out, but his own weariness of life. His gift was a furious one, but barren; writing much, he repeated himself so joylessly that in the end he seemed to be mocking himself with the same quiet viciousness with which, even as a boy, he had mocked the universe. An old child, it was not merely by his somberness that he anticipated the misanthropy of the twentieth-century novel. Pride and a fiercely quaking splendor mark his first and last apotheosis: he was the first great tragic figure in the modern American generation.

CHRISTOPHER BENFY ON HENRY FLEMING'S INITIATION TO WAR AND MANHOOD

The Red Badge of Courage is indeed about an initiation, though not necessarily into manhood. What Crane tried to imagine in *The Red Badge*, and what repeatedly captured his attention when he came to experience real war, was the fate of the body in human conflict. To put it another way, Crane found no better place than war to show the alarming fact—alarming to him and to his hero Henry Fleming—that human beings have bodies, and are therefore mortal. (Perhaps it's worth remembering here that the household in which Crane grew up was a place of physical denial—no dancing, smoking, or drinking.) This may seem like a small or self-evident or peculiar discovery to make on the battleground—one made more easily and pleasantly on the playground. And indeed Crane did often compare his vision of war with his experience in sports, telling one correspondent soon after the publication of the novel that "I have never been in a battle, but I believe that I got my sense of the rage of conflict on the football field." But war presented obvious opportunities for opening up the human body for exploration. *The Red Badge of Courage* can be read as a series of confrontations, of increasing intensity, with human corporeality, as Henry Fleming is awakened to the fact of his own physical existence.

The novel begins with an army that is all body and a private who is all mind: the task of Crane's narrative is to unite them. The famous opening paragraph envisions the army as itself a great body in the process of awakening.

> The cold passed reluctantly from the earth, and the retiring fogs revealed an army stretched out on the hills, resting. As the landscape changed from brown to green, the army awakened, and began to tremble with eagerness at the noise of rumors. It cast its eyes upon the roads, which were growing from long troughs of liquid mud to proper thoroughfares. A river, amber-tinted in the shadow of its banks, purled at the army's feet; and at night, when the stream had become of a sorrowful blackness, one could see across it the red, eyelike gleam of hostile camp-fires set in the low brows of distant hills.

The first two sentences establish the pattern for how Crane will divide his episodes throughout the novel. It is by means of fade-ins and fade-outs, dissipating fogs and gathering haze, that Crane makes his transitions. The equally famous and often maligned last sentence of the novel—it doesn't occur in the manuscript, and may have been an editor's suggestion—has seemed to some critics to strike a major note of cheer in what should be a minor ending. In fact it merely completes the pattern: "Over the river a golden ray of sun came through the hosts of leaden rain clouds." Such verbal alchemy, gold out of lead, is typical of the high polish of Crane's prose, as he steers his private through a series of baffling scenes. The fogs and hazes often seem as much inner as outer weather, for Fleming is constantly trying to clear his head to make sense of what is happening to him.

It is often said that Crane's novel takes the perspective of an ordinary soldier, an observation that has been made repeatedly in recent comparisons of *The Red Badge* to various films based on the Vietnam War. But Henry Fleming is not ordinary. Crane introduces him as a sort of budding intellectual who spends much of his time lying on his bunk or on the ground thinking. Amid the confusing rumors and predictions in the opening scene, the "youthful private" wants above all a quiet place in which to reflect.

> After receiving a fill of discussions concerning marches and attacks, he went through his hut and crawled through an intricate hole that served it as a door. He wished to be alone with some new thoughts that had lately come to him.

It is privacy that Fleming is after, and Crane's preliminary title for the novel was "*Private* Fleming / His various battles."

In the opening scenes, Private Fleming is a disembodied mind consumed by thinking. He doesn't conceive of war as involving wounding and dying. Instead, he thinks of it as an abstract sequence of doubts, demonstrations, and proofs. He lies in his bunk pondering his "serious problem": "He tried to mathematically prove to himself that he would not run from a battle." Fleming's greatest fear is of humiliation. He's not afraid that he'll go forward to his death, but backwards to his shame.

But the fear of shame and the fear of death are of course related, the one in effect masking the other. For what Fleming at the outset of the novel is afraid of is to own—or to own up to—his own body. To be embodied is to carry your own death around with you. Only when Fleming has been initiated into this mystery can he show true courage. The physicality of the title points to this lesson, for the red badge is a wound, and courage is, as the root of the word suggests, a matter of the organ that pumps the blood.

Fleming's need for convincing proof of his own courage can only be satisfied by a wound. This association of wounds with doubt and verification has a long foreground in Western culture. Jacob's wounding in the Old Testament indicates the existence of an unseen God. Christ's wounds on the cross verify his mortality, just as his wounds after the resurrection prove, to doubting Thomas, his divinity. Crane invokes biblical scenes of verification-by-wounding at several key points in the novel.

Crane orchestrates Fleming's progress in and out of battle as an education in wounds and corpses. Accounts of the novel, in their attention to its "psychological truth," tend to overlook how physical the novel is in its focus, how minutely concerned with details of the fate of the body in war—its characteristic gestures, its gait, its pervasive vulnerability, its contorted positions in death. As in other war writings, the first view of a corpse, as the army marches toward the battlefield, is a critical moment, and Crane lingers over it.

> Once the line encountered the body of a dead soldier. He lay upon his back staring at the sky. He was dressed in an awkward suit of yellowish brown. The youth could see that the soles of his shoes had been worn to the thinness of writing paper, and from a great rent in one the dead foot projected piteously. And it was as if fate had betrayed the soldier. In death it exposed to his enemies that poverty which in life he had perhaps concealed from his friends.

Death is here conceived of as the ultimate violation of privacy, as though the rending of the body reveals the mind's secrets.

> The youth looked keenly at the ashen face. The wind raised the tawny beard. It moved as if a hand were stroking it. He vaguely desired to walk around and around the body and stare; the impulse of the living to try to read in dead eyes the answer to the Question.

As Henry continues to wrestle with his problem, he encounters a series of wounded men, as though to find out by what processes men are turned into corpses.

Henry's regiment eventually reaches the battlefield and is involved in intense fighting. Many of the soldiers flee in panic, including Henry. After this ignoble retreat, the earlier sequence of an encounter with a corpse followed by a parade of wounded men is repeated, but this time with far greater intensity. In one of the most celebrated and uncanny scenes in the novel, Henry stumbles through the woods until he reaches "a place where the high, arching boughs made a chapel." What follows is a sort of sacred rite, an initiation into the mysteries.

> He softly pushed the green doors aside and entered. Pine needles were a gentle brown carpet. There was a religious half light.
>
> Near the threshold he stopped, horror-stricken at the sight of a thing.
>
> He was being looked at by a dead man who was seated with his back against a columnlike tree. The corpse was dressed in a uniform that once had been blue, but was now faded to a melancholy shade of green. The eyes, staring at the youth, had changed to the dull hue to be seen on the side of a dead fish. The mouth was open. Its red had changed to an appalling yellow. Over the gray skin of the face ran little ants. One was trundling some sort of a bundle along the upper lip.

Each detail—the faded, green uniform, the dull hue of the eyes, the busy ants—draws this corpse back into the natural landscape, as if to prove that the body returns to dust.

> The youth gave a shriek as he confronted the thing. He was for moments turned to stone before it. He remained staring into the liquid-looking eyes. The dead man and the living man exchanged a long look. Then the youth cautiously put one hand behind him and brought it against a tree. Leaning upon this he retreated, step

by step, with his face still toward the thing. He feared that if he turned his back the body might spring up and stealthily pursue him.

The sense here of a man looking into a mirror is palpable, from the long look exchanged with the liquid-like eyes to the reflected gesture of leaning against a tree. The passage gains in intensity from the eerie stasis of the scene, with the "religious half light" of the chapel and the Medusa-like power of the corpse to turn its confronter to stone. The mystery into which Henry Fleming is being initiated is the fact of his own embodiedness. The real lesson to be learned in this chapel is not the lesson of courage but the lesson of corporeality—and thence mortality.

Like doubting Thomas, Fleming longs to touch the corpse, to experience the fact of the body: "His unguided feet ... caught aggravatingly in brambles; and with it all he received a subtle suggestion to touch the corpse. As he thought of his hand upon it he shuddered profoundly." After the scene in the wooded chapel, Henry experiences "the steady current of the maimed" with greater intensity, and a deeper understanding of how "the torn bodies expressed the awful machinery in which the men had been entangled."

And now occurs one of the strangest sections of the novel, for Henry, unhurt himself but burdened with the new knowledge of the chapel, begins to envy the wounded. His own intact body becomes an embarrassment to him, and in his new awareness of his body he thinks his shame is visible. "Where yeh hit?" asks one of the wounded men, a "tattered soldier."

> "Why," began the youth, "I—I—that is—why—I—"
> He turned away suddenly and slid through the crowd. His brow was heavily flushed, and his fingers were picking nervously at one of his buttons.

His body has become the expression of his soul, and from blushing he progresses to a fantasy of his body as a legible text.

But he was amid wounds. The mob of men was bleeding. Because of the tattered soldier's question he now felt that his shame could be viewed. He was continually casting sidelong glances to see if the men were contemplating the letters of guilt he felt burned into his brow.

At times he regarded the wounded soldiers in an envious way. He conceived persons with torn bodies to be peculiarly happy. He wished that he, too, had a wound, a red badge of courage.

Two more scenes complete Fleming's initiation into the fate of the body in war. The parade of the wounded culminates in Fleming's encounter with his old friend Jim Conklin, who is severely wounded in the side and about to die. The whole passage is shockingly physical, with Conklin behaving like "a devotee of a mad religion, blood-sucking, muscle-wrenching, bone-crushing." Henry finds himself miming each of Conklin's agonies, as though he's learning about his own body and its capacity for pain:

> Turning his head swiftly, the youth saw his friend running in a staggering and stumbling way toward a little clump of bushes. His heart seemed to wrench itself almost free from his body at this sight. He made a noise of pain.

A moment later, Conklin begins to have trouble breathing.

> The chest of the doomed soldier began to heave with a strained motion. It increased in violence until it was as if an animal was within and was kicking and tumbling furiously to be free.
>
> This spectacle of gradual strangulation made the youth writhe, and once as his friend rolled his eyes, he saw something in them that made him sink wailing to the ground.

Finally, Conklin collapses:

A swift muscular contortion made the left shoulder strike the ground first.

The body seemed to bounce a little way from the earth....

The youth had watched, spellbound, this ceremony at the place of meeting. His face had been twisted into an expression of every agony he had imagined for his friend.

He now sprang to his feet and, going closer, gazed upon the pastelike face. The mouth was open and the teeth showed in a laugh.

As the flap of the blue jacket fell away from the body, he could see that the side looked as if it had been chewed by wolves.

That last detail, borrowed perhaps from a story by Ambrose Bierce, where the wolves are not metaphorical, could hardly stress more starkly the physical ravages of war.

As Fleming mirrors in his own gestures the contortions of his friend's body, he is learning about his own capacity for pain and death. As J. Glenn Gray has observed in *The Warriors*, his memoir and meditation on men in battle,

When the belief in one's indestructibility is due to a defect of imagination, other experiences than being wounded may suffice to waken the soldier to his situation. It may be the death of an acquaintance in his arms, where the transition between life and death is made imaginatively visible for the first time....

Such is the strange logic of Henry's initiation that when he does receive his wound, his "red badge of courage," the ironic circumstances seem almost beside the point. The scene is a vivid, if somewhat disguised, reworking of Jacob wrestling with the angel/man at Peniel—one of the central biblical scenes of wounding as verification. Henry clutches one of the retreating Union soldiers by the arm, and they swing around "face to face." "Why—why—" Fleming stammers as the man screams, "Let go me! Let go me!" Instead of a blessing, the man gives

Fleming a blow to the head, and he stumbles about "like a babe trying to walk." He is inundated by a rush of intensely physical memories, "certain meals his mother had cooked at home," and "how he and his companions used to go from the school-house to the bank of a shaded pool":

> He saw his clothes in disorderly array upon the grass of the bank. He felt the swash of the fragrant water upon his body.

Finally a fatherly soldier turns up who cheerily questions Fleming "like one manipulating the mind of a child," and he drops Fleming off at the campsite of his regiment.

The succession of scenes has a hallucinatory quality, and yet an inescapable logic. The recurring themes, especially in the last two scenes, suggest a religious meditation, by this son of a Methodist minister, on God the Father who won't answer "Why?" and perhaps a personal memory as well, on the death of his own father. But the lost child searching for a safe haven is also part of a thread running through Crane's work and life: the search for a private refuge from various kinds of exposure.

We are made to feel that Fleming has undergone a profound change between his flight from battle in the first part of the book and his conspicuous heroism in the second. The scenes of initiation have worked this transformation. If there is a letdown in imaginative vividness in the last third of the book, as I believe there is, it may be because Henry's education about the body is at an end.

But at the conclusion of the book, Crane turns once more to the fate of the body. As he moves his private out of battle, Crane's biblical phrasing lingers for a moment on the healing scars.

> So it came to pass that as he trudged from the place of blood and wrath his soul changed. He came from hot plowshares to prospects of clover tranquilly, and it was as if hot plowshares were not. Scars faded as flowers.

It rained. The procession of weary soldiers became a bedraggled train, despondent and muttering, marching with churning effort in a trough of liquid brown mud under a low, wretched sky. Yet the youth smiled, for he saw that the world was a world for him, though many discovered it to be made of oaths and walking sticks. He had rid himself of the red sickness of battle. The sultry nightmare was in the past. He had been an animal blistered and sweating in the heat and pain of war. He turned now with a lover's thirst to images of tranquil skies, fresh meadows, cool brooks—an existence of soft and eternal peace.

Over the river a golden ray of sun came through the hosts of leaden rain clouds.

By treating Fleming's emergence from battle as the recovery from disease, Crane uses the most intensely physical metaphor he can think of. Fleming's wish for tranquility in the closing sentences has sometimes been taken to be Crane's ironic summing up of Fleming's naive hopes. But it also reads, perhaps unconsciously, as a longing for death—what the poet James Merrill has called "the country of a thousand years of peace." The enigmatic sentence "Scars faded as flowers" moves in two directions: to be like a flower is to live in beauty, but a fading flower is rapidly approaching death. To be fully at home in the body is to find "that the world is a world for [us]" and one that we can love with "a lover's thirst." But it is also to acknowledge that our lives are, like the flowers, finite. We are forever scarred by our own impending death.

LINDA H. DAVIS ON CRANE'S ORIGINALITY WITH LITERARY ANTECEDENTS

The story of young Henry Fleming's trial by artillery fire in the Civil War was not radically new in subject matter; it echoed familiar themes and details of plot long available, though there is no telling whether Stephen had read any of the war stories of

Zola, Frank Wilkeson, or Joseph Kirkland. These authors and others had written about war in brutally realistic narratives and tackled the subject of fear and cowardice in wartime. Some had written about war from the perspective of the private soldier—notably Wilkeson, in *Recollections of a Private Soldier in the Army of the Potomac*, and Warren Lee Goss, whose "Recollections of a Private" appeared in the *Century*. A book titled *Corporal Si Klegg and his "Pard,"* by Wilbur F. Hinman, chronicled the metamorphosis of a farm boy into a war veteran; marked with heavy dialect, it showed a young soldier wrestling with doubts about his courage, who later takes the flag from the hands of an injured standard bearer. These details also reappeared, yet were made new, in Stephen's novel.

One could pick up ideas anywhere. On Sunday, February 12, 1893, the month before Stephen started reading the old *Centurys*, the *New York Times* published a Civil War story called "The Coward" above the initials "C.G.S." This piece of hackwork tells of a young Yankee soldier named Jamie Mayhew, whose first engagement comes at Vicksburg. Ridiculed as a "sissy," Jamie begs his sergeant to release him from fighting. "I will die if I have to go; I am a fearful coward!" he cries. The sergeant refuses, insisting that he is sick, not afraid, but Jamie manages to slip behind the front ranks anyway and flee, leaving many of his regiment to die. Like Henry Fleming, he ends up in a wood, where he feels safe from the action, but he worries about being shot for desertion. Captured by the enemy and forced to accompany them on their nocturnal raids, Jamie eventually redeems himself by warning the Union soldiers about a coming raid. He is wounded while making his way back to them, but he recovers and becomes a great hero, and eventually a minister, beloved by his congregation.

If Stephen borrowed ideas for his plot, he made them utterly his own. In style, treatment, and perspective, his war tale suggests no other, with the exception of Tolstoy's *Sebastopol*. Tolstoy is the only war writer he is known to have read, "the writer I admire most of all." *Sebastopol*, consisting of three nonfiction essays chronicling the defense of the Russian city during the Crimean War, seems to have most influenced

Stephen's thinking or at least amplified it. The fledgling war writer found much to which he could respond in Tolstoy's book, which was available to Americans in an 1887 translation from the French by Frank D. Millet. Distinguished by graphic realism, an unremitting clinical view of wounded and dead men, and an unromantic depiction of war as a "house of pain," the essays Tolstoy wrote in his twenties claimed "truth" as their "hero"—something Stephen Crane might have said of his own story.

Tolstoy had showed how men *feel* in battle. His approach was impressionistic and ironic; he linked flowers with corpses, addressed man's vanity and self-delusion, and sympathized with the common man—all hallmarks of Crane's work. Having seen war firsthand, the Russian writer understood that in battle, men lose part of themselves. The young officer described in this passage from *Sebastopol* sounds, in the beginning, very much like Henry Fleming.

> The feeling of this desertion in the presence of danger, of death, as he believed, oppressed his heart with the glacial weight of a stone. Halting in the middle of the place, he looked all about him to see if he was observed, and taking his head in both hands, he murmured, with a voice broken by terror, "My God! am I really a despicable poltroon, a coward, I who have lately dreamed of dying for my country, for my Czar, and that with joy! Yes, I am an unfortunate and despicable being!" he cried, in profound despair, and quite undeceived about himself. Having finally overcome his emotion, he asked the sentinel to show him the house of the commander of the battery.

Tolstoy's war was grounded in reality. Stephen Crane's portrait of war, seen as an assault on the senses, was stunningly original. Not even the great Tolstoy had done this. Stephen imagined Henry Fleming's battle as a psychological and spiritual crisis. It is not the Confederate army on which Henry's fear focuses but nature, alternately friendly, hostile, and indifferent, which the youth sees through the distorting lens of his vanity and his ego. "The world was fully interested in other matters," Stephen wrote. A stream regards Henry with "white bubble eyes"; armies attack each other in "panther-fashion." Stephen drew on his religious upbringing and the violent rhetoric that had terrified him as a child to paint nature. Here, in "the cathedral light of the forest," the trees sang "a hymn of twilight," and the insects quieted in "a devotional pause." Lamblike eyes and "fierce-eyed hosts" peered from the forest. "War, the blood-swollen god" was fought in a "celestial battle," and "the chorus pealed over the still earth." "It seemed that there would shortly be an encounter of strange beaks and claws, as of eagles," Stephen wrote, harking back to the eagles of the Book of Revelations. Having' returned to his regiment to fight, Henry "felt the daring spirit of a savage, religion-mad." He became a "war devil," he "had fought like a pagan who defends his religion."

Stephen mocked Henry's delusions with an ironic narrative, while letting what he later called the red devils in his own heart loose upon the page. In his celestial battle the youth saw demons, imps, and "swirling battle-phantoms." The fires of hell burned in the crimson rays of war, which made "weird and satanic effects." Soldiers in combat appeared as fiends with "black faces and glowing eyes." Henry heard the battle as a "furnace-roar." "The flames bit him," Stephen wrote, and the men of the regiment "stood as men tied to stakes." He used his natural feeling for color, his palette of reds, black, and yellow, to create some of his most conspicuous effects. Stephen told Frank Noxon that a passage in Goethe which "analysed the effect" of certain colors on "the human mind" influenced him. Red—the color of blood and fire—best expressed his feelings. Henry Fleming saw campfires as "red, peculiar blossoms." He experienced "the red sickness of battle." Influenced, perhaps unconsciously, by Kipling as well as Goethe, Stephen ended Chapter Nine with the sentence "the red sun was pasted in the sky like a wafer."[1]

In part, it is the insistence of the novel's religious imagery, which was both conscious and unwitting, that stamps it as the work of Stephen Crane. He could no more escape the religion that was in him than he could change his eye color or his bone structure. In creating the character of Fleming, he kept close to what he knew—to his honesty, as he would put it. He gave the youth his own eyes. He embraced his religious heritage while railing against it and controlling it with irony. Writing from within to show "war from within," he made the experience seem true.

Henry Fleming carried Stephen into the deepest part of himself. During a pivotal scene, Henry finds himself in a little sanctuary in the woods. Bathed in "a religious half-light," the sheltering bower welcomes him with a "religion of peace." "He conceived nature to be a woman with a deep aversion to tragedy," wrote Stephen. Then Henry parts the green doors of his sanctuary to be confronted by a corpse in a Union army uniform, a "thing" with "liquid-looking eyes." Black ants trundle over the gray face, "venturing horribly near to the eyes." As he flees the green chapel, Henry imagines that the dead man will rise "and squawk after him in horrible menaces." The fascination with the corpse's face, with what happens to the body after death turns up in other scenes and images, in the upturned, "corpse-hued faces" of stricken soldiers, in the youth's first encounter with a dead soldier, at whom he longs to stare. The corpse is tawny-haired, like the author, and poor, the soles of his shoes "worn to the thinness of writing paper."

And so Stephen had arrived at himself. He would tell Linson that the tale was "the product of an utter discouragement, almost of despair." He thought it "a pity that art should be a child of pain, and yet I think it is." The pictures of dead soldiers reflected Stephen's sense of himself as puny and not long for this world—a self-image compounded and complicated by the early religious assault upon his senses, which was like a melody he could not get out of his head.

For Henry Fleming there was no easy heroism. Though the youth ultimately conformed to Victorian notions of duty and honor—a large part of what defined a man—his desertion in the field haunted him. He had no sustaining religious faith to comfort him, as other Civil War soldiers had, no Christian fatalism, no sense of true salvation. "He had been to touch the great death, and found that, after all, it was but the great death," Stephen wrote. "Scars faded as flowers." Much later, after he thought he had finished the novel, he added an ironic last line to show that Henry's dreams of eternal peace were the same old delusions. Nature would have the last word: "Over the river a golden ray of sun came through the hosts of leaden rain clouds." The last line of Tolstoy's "Sebastopol in December, 1854" also begins with an image of the sun shining through gray clouds above the ocean.[2] Perhaps more suggestively, in Helen Crane's tribute to Stephen's dead father, she had written in closing, "And so we laid his body away under the evergreens, amid the scenes of his childhood, as a flood of golden sunshine burst upon the scene."

Notes

1. In *The Light That Failed* (1891), Rudyard Kipling described the shining sun as "a blood-red wafer, on the water."

2. "Day closes; the sun, disappearing at the horizon, shines through the gray clouds which surround it, and lights up with purple rays the rippling sea."

BEN SATTERFIELD ON THE NOVEL AS HUMANISTIC WORK OF ART

To offer yet another contribution to the interpretation of "so notoriously overanalyzed a novel" as *The Red Badge of Courage* is to invite the charge of performing a dispensable act. But just the opposite is true: a coherent and uncontradictory reading is necessary. This short novel by Stephen Crane has engendered critical and expository schisms of so profound a nature that there is not even common agreement as to what the book is about; in form, it is generally labeled a novel of initiation, a *Bildungsroman*, but in content, it has been called everything from a negative and dehumanized portrait of pessimistic-deterministic philosophy to an inspiring religious allegory. In fact, *The Red Badge*, while neither plotless nor obscure, remains something of an enigma on any level other than that of a war story, in spite of its having been pored over by myriad critics. My intention here is to present a tenable analysis that views the book as a consistent and unified work of art that is neither allegorical nor naturalistic, but essentially affirmative and humanistic in scope.

(...)

Since Crane relies so heavily upon it, imagery will be stressed as a key to meaning, with particular emphasis on animal imagery, the abundance of which makes it impossible to read the novel without being constantly aware of it. Although this imagery has been repeatedly cited, its dominance is not yet apparent to all. In the Stephen Crane issue of the *University of Minnesota Pamphlets on American Writers*, Jean Cazemajou's insistence is that "religious imagery prevails" in *The Red Badge of Courage*. Following this declaration, a few examples are quoted, including "the ghost of his flight," "columnlike," and "the tattered man." These meager and dubious examples are then subsequently and inaccurately referred to as a "procession of religious images."

Most of the images in this novel are not religious in any recognizable sense; indeed, one would have to expand the definition of "religious" beyond credible limits to include "a specter of reproach" and "the creed of soldiers" as phrases appropriate to its meaning. The animal imagery, however, is not doubtful and permeates the novel. The first definite allusions occur in chapter one where the recruits are referred to as "prey" and "fresh fish," and the same type of imagery persists through the final chapter where one particular officer is described as a "whale"—an image that recalls the "fish" of chapter one. But despite the fact that over seventy comparisons of the men to animals have been counted in *The Red Badge of Courage* and one article has been written solely about animal imagery (in which is stated: "Excluding all the numerous sunken metaphors which imply animal-like action, this short novel contains at least 80 figures of speech employing animals or their characteristics"), this imagery has not been adequately explained nor its coherence demonstrated. The often noted (and I believe mistaken) interpretation of the animal imagery is that it reinforces Crane's "naturalism."

Donald Pease on History and Heroic Attributes

In the April 1896 issue of *The Dial*, Army General A.C. McClurg, in a critical document interesting less for the general's insight into the novel than the direction of his criticism of it, bitterly denounced *The Red Badge of Courage* as a vicious satire of army life. "The hero of the book, if such he can be called, was an ignorant and stupid country lad without a spark of patriotic feeling or soldierly ambition," the general wrote. "He is throughout an idiot or a maniac and betrays no trace of the reasoning being. No thrill of patriotic devotion to cause or country ever moves his breast, and not even an emotion of manly courage."

(...)

Clearly Crane inflamed the general's ire by leaving political considerations out of his account altogether. Written at a time when the nation's historians were characterizing the political and ideological significance of seemingly every battle in the war, Crane's power derived from his decision to reverse the procedure. By stripping the names from the battles he describes, Crane releases the sheer force of the battle incidents unrelieved by their assimilation into a historical narrative frame. And like a naïve social historian, General McClurg decided to make good on the debits in Crane's account. In his critical relation to the war novel he restored to the narrative what Crane carefully eliminated from Henry Fleming's confrontation with war: a political and moral frame of reference.

(...)

General McClurg in his review, then, did not wish to launch a personal attack on Private Fleming but to recover those representations Stephen Crane had withheld. As the general's review vividly attests, by 1896 these representations had become ingrained enough in the American character for one of her "representative men" to take their absence as a personal affront.

By mentioning General McClurg's reaction specifically, I do not mean to isolate its eccentricity, but to suggest that in its very force his reaction represents the urgent need to recover that sense of a developing American character Crane's account has taken leave of. Whether commentators attack this lack of character directly as General McClurg does in denouncing Private Fleming as a coward, or denounce it after a manner subtle enough to remain unconscious of it, as do more recent critics, by reading a coherent line of character development into the arbitrary incidents in Henry's life, the wish remains the same in both cases, to recover the sense of exemplary continuity, integrity, and significance for those Civil War events Stephen Crane has forcibly excised from official history. Crane acknowledges the urgency of this need by never failing to drive a wedge between the sheer contingency of Henry's battle experiences and those reflections on them that never account for so much as they displace these incidents with other concerns. What results is an ongoing sense of disorientation, a knowledge of Henry Fleming's involvement in a battle that history will later turn into a monumental event, but whose dimensions never presently convert into anything more than a series of discontinuous incidents, followed by pauses whose emptiness Henry can never fill with sufficient reflections.

GIORGIO MARIANI ON THE IDEAL AND THE ACTUAL IN FLEMING'S WAR EXPERIENCE

At the beginning of the novel we learn that Henry "had dreamed of battles all his life—of vague and bloody conflicts ... he had long despaired of witnessing a Greeklike struggle. Such would be no more he said. Men were better, or more timid. Secular and religious education had effaced the throat grappling instinct, or else firm finance held in check the passions."[22] One way to read this passage, and the rest of the novel, is to distinguish between Henry's values, his fantasies of Homeric battles, and what war really is, with its violence and brutality. *The Red Badge* would then be the story of how one becomes a man only after seeing through the fallacy of traditions and stereotypes. The problem with this reading is that if in the course of the novel Henry gains some kind of insight into the nature of war, he does so not by rejecting brutality and violence, but through them. It is by becoming a "war devil" that Henry also becomes able, as the narrator tells us, "to study his deeds, his failures, and his achievements," and "to criticise them with some correctness." By the end, Henry may have some doubts as to the adequacy of "the brass and bombast of his earlier gospels" (108), but he does not question the value of his war experience as such. On the other hand, if we believe that in the last chapter Henry is still deluding himself, we must also conclude that it is his failure to mature that the narrative condemns, not his "barbarian" (80) behavior.

I would suggest, however, that Crane's irony may to a degree undercut Henry's fantasies of Homeric struggles, but not the force of the throat-grappling instinct. This remains a source of interest and fascination throughout the novel. Henry's initial interest in war is voyeuristic: "He had read of marches, sieges, conflicts, and he had longed to see it all.... His busy mind had drawn for him large pictures extravagant in color, lurid with breathless deeds" (3). Henry's decision to enlist is sparked by his desire to become part of the public spectacle of war. When he realizes that "almost every day the newspapers printed accounts of a decisive victory" (3) he wants to have the chance to perform on this exciting stage. But Henry does not abandon the idea that war is a thrilling theatrical experience after he enlists. The longing to "see it all" will continue to dominate his thoughts throughout the novel. Moreover we soon discover that his comrades share his longing. This is how Crane describes the moments before the first skirmish: "The youth looked at the men nearest him, and saw, for the most part, expressions of deep interest, as if they were investigating something that had fascinated them.... They were going to look at war, the red animal—war, the blood-swollen god" (18–19). The theatrical metaphor is again picked up a few pages later, in a remarkable scene: "There were moments of waiting. The youth thought of the village street at home before the arrival of the circus parade on a day of spring.... Some one cried 'Here they come!'" (25). The final exclamation blends together the circus and war; appropriately Jim Conklin will later remark about the battle, "Lord, what a circus!" (43).

Even in the midst of fierce fighting, the regiment is described as totally absorbed by the spectacle of war:

> The men, halted, had the opportunity to see some of their comrades dropping with moans and shrieks. A few lay under foot, still or wailing. And now for an instant the men stood, their rifles slack in their hands, and watched the regiment dwindle. They appeared dazed and stupid. This spectacle seemed to paralyze them, overcome them with total fascination. They stared woodenly at the sights, and, lowering their eyes, looked from face to face. (86)

The desire to *see*, to completely surrender oneself to the aesthetics of violence and horror, may transform the soldiers into "stupid" automata but also keeps them firmly entrenched in the battlefield and fuels their desire to continue the fight. Similarly, at the peak of his triumph as flagbearer, Henry stands in the midst of action "deeply absorbed as a spectator," and it is precisely thanks to such mindless fascination with what is taking place before his eyes that he experiences no fear. "He did not know that he breathed; that the flag hung silently over him, so absorbed was he" (99).

After his flight, what prompts Henry to return to the battlefield is the desire to be the spectator of a "celestial battle." The mythical perception of the enemy army as a "red and green monster" is first counterbalanced, and finally overcome, by an irresistible desire to look at the theater of war. "The battle was like the grinding of an immense and terrible machine to him. Its complexities and powers, its grim processes, fascinated him. He must go close and see it produce corpses" (39). Henry is attracted to war as if it were a football game: "A certain mothlike quality kept him in the vicinity of the battle. He had a great desire to see, and to get news. He wished to know who was winning" (52). The fascination with the martial spectacle produces, in its turn, the desire to become an active part of the show, so that Henry's "growth" signals not a refusal of the ideology of spectacle but its utmost triumph. It is certainly no accident that the youth feels the "quiver of war desire" immediately after he thinks of the sublimity of "getting calmly killed on a high place before the eyes of all" (51). The narrator may ironically undercut Henry's fantasies of returning home "to make the hearts of the people glow with stories of war.... He saw his gaping audience picturing him as the central figure in blazing scenes" (73). Yet what the narrative delivers is precisely Henry's apotheosis as an actor on the stage of war. Although he is not killed in front of his audience, part of Henry's dream comes true when, after fighting like a "beast," he turns towards his comrades only to discover that "they seemed all engaged in staring with astonishment at him. They had become spectators" (80).

The spectacular rhetoric of *Red Badge* has been analyzed by Amy Kaplan, who has also noted the important fact that it is not only Henry and his comrades who make sense of their war experience through the language of theatrical performance. Kaplan believes that Crane himself, "by focusing not on politics but on the problem of representing war ... transforms the representation of war from a shared experience that can be narrated in written or oral stories into an exotic spectacle that must be viewed by a spectator and conveyed to an audience".[23] If on the one hand the reader looks at war, for the most part, through Henry's eyes, on the other the narrator too insists on presenting war as a spectacle performed in front of an audience who enjoys it, or at least looks at it with curiosity.[24] By often characterizing the battlefield as a "stage" or a "scene," and the soldiers as football players or "sprinters," the narrator invites the reader to regard the events depicted in "spectator fashion," a phrase that is used late in the novel to describe the way Henry mentally reviews his "performances" on the battleground.

I agree with Kaplan's general description of *Red Badge* as a text that, contrary to what has often been claimed, does not replace the chivalric fantasies that crowded the world of contemporary popular romances (and of Henry's own mind) with a more accurate description of reality but instead "frames a new sense of the real as a highly mediated spectacle".[25] However, her claim that Crane's representational strategy "both adopt[s] and subvert[s]" the martial ideal, or that the novel both "implicitly contributes to and criticizes the contemporary militarization of American culture" ignores the ideological implications of Crane's representational strategy.[26] Crane's spectacular rhetorics, I believe, can be better understood if seen as aiming to recode or rewrite the world of war "in terms of perception as a semi-autonomous activity."[27]

In so far as it makes of the instantaneousness of sight the main tool for reading the world, Crane's recreation of war as spectacle functions as a stylistic and narrative machinery devoted to the containment of the historical and political reality of war.[28] It projects, in other words, an imaginary—that is, an ideological—resolution of a concrete social problem. Now ideology can, and probably always must, accommodate quite different impulses and desires, but it is obviously incapable of criticizing itself. As Terry Eagleton remarks, "strictly speaking there can be no contradiction *within* ideology, since its function is precisely to eradicate it. There can be contradiction only between ideology and what it occludes—history itself."[29] Given that, as Kaplan herself notes, history—i.e., the "real"—is nowhere present in the novel except in the form of spectacle, one is left to wonder where Crane's critical perspective on war is to be located.[30] Moreover, as Eagleton continues, history should not be conceived as an ultimate bedrock of reality which forces the literary text to unveil the mystery of its ideology. The contradictions implicated within its ideological system "may be forced from it by its historically determined encounter with another ideology, or ideological sub-ensemble."[31] In other words the martial ideal can be called into question only by resorting to a different ideological formation.

One can, for example, unmask war as the product of a social dynamics that ultimately favors the ruling classes, or attack it on ethical and moral grounds from an uncompromising pacifist perspective. Yet *Red Badge* nowhere articulates either these or any other anti-war discourses. One may wish to say that Henry's self-delusion and confusion prove that the spectacular apprehension of war is both epistemologically and ethically flawed because it prevents him from seeing what war "really is." The fact is, however, that the text does not provide access to a hypothetical authorial view of the true meaning of war. We may dislike the idea of war being a form of aesthetic entertainment, but this is the *only* way in which the text knows war.

Notes

22. Stephen Crane, *The Red Badge of Courage*, p. 3. Further page references will be included parenthetically in the text.

23. Amy Kaplan, "The Spectacle of War," in *New Essays*, p. 79. My understanding of the historical and political significance of Crane's spectacular rhetorics, however, differs from hers. Lee Clark Mitchell has also addressed the abundance of "visual activity" in the novel; see his "The Spectacle of Character in Crane's *Red Badge of Courage*," *Determined Fictions: American Literary Naturalism* (New York: Columbia University Press, 1989), pp. 96–116.

24. Though he does not comment on the historical or political significance of Crane's "impressionism," Sergio Perosa notes that "verbs like *to see, perceive, look, observe, gaze, witness, watch, stare, peer, cast eyes, discover* etc. appear on practically every page, indeed, no less than 350 times in this fairly short novel" ("Naturalism and Impressionism in Stephen Crane's Fiction," in *Stephen Crane: A Collection of Critical Essays*, p. 87).

25. Kaplan, p. 95.

26. Ibid., pp. 95, 79.

27. This is how Jameson characterizes Joseph Conrad's *"aestheticizing strategy"*—a strategy which, like Impressionism, "discards even the operative fiction of some interest in the constituted objects of the natural world, and offers the exercise of perception and the perceptual recombination of sense data as an end in itself" (*The Political Unconscious*, pp. 229–30). My notion of Crane's spectacular strategy is indebted to Jameson's analysis of Conrad, who, it should not be forgotten, was a close friend and great admirer of Stephen

Crane, whom he once defined as "*the only impressionist* and *only* an impressionist" (as quoted by Joseph Nagel, *Stephen Crane and Literary Impressionism* [University Park, Pennsylvania: The Pennsylvania State University Press, 1980], p. 1. Emphasis in the original).

28. Dana B. Polan writes that "The world of spectacle is a world without background, a world in which things only exist or mean in the way they appear.... The will-to-spectacle is the assertion that a world of foreground is the only world that matters or is the only world that *is*" ("'Above all else to make you see': Cinema and the Ideology of Spectacle," *Boundary* 2, 11 [1982–83], p. 135).

29. Terry Eagleton, *Criticism and Ideology* (London: New Left Books, 1976), p. 95.

30. Paul Virilio has argued that "along the 'war machine' there has always existed an ocular (and later optical and electro-optical) 'watching machine' capable of providing soldiers, and particularly commanders, with a visual perspective on the military action under way. From the original watch-tower through the anchored balloon to the reconnaissance aircraft and remote-sensing satellites, one and the same function has been indefinitely repeated, the eye's function being the function of a weapon" (*War and Cinema: The Logistics of Perception* [London: Verso, 1989], p. 3). Virilio's argument reinforces my skepticism concerning the supposed critical dimension of Crane's spectacle of war. If, as Virilio maintains, the scope of war is to produce itself as a spectacle, *Red Badge* overlaps with, rather than resists, this need. Crane's representation of war depends on the sense which, according to Virilio, war exalts over all others.

31. Eagleton, p. 96.

David Halliburton on Crane's Use of Color

Reportorial color, indicating a phenomenal base in ordinary experience, appears in the opening passage where the landscape changes from brown to green, the river is amber-tinted, the night black, and the camp fires red.[15] Later, guns make "grey clouds" (II, 100) and the gray of Confederate uniforms contrasts with the Union blue; and so on. Reportorial technique, in other words, registers how a color immediately appears.

Some instances turn the perceptual screw, however; such is the case with "The red sun was pasted in the sky like a wafer" (II, 58). Now, the reader has no reason to suspect that the sun was not red: Red, as a solar hue, has been accepted since

Anglo-Saxon times (*OED* A.I.1.c., 450). But its location in a metonymic chain of reds tints it, as it were, so that the color of the sun takes on overtones from, say, the protagonist's red rage, or the red sickness of battle. Further from the phenomenal base are "the flashing points of yellow and red" (II, 120) that penetrate a wall of smoke. Although points of such color may well appear on a battlefield, explosions from artillery are not typically in primary colors: This yellow looks suspiciously like Goethe's paradigmatic yellow and the red looks equally pure. In general, colors in Crane combine the degrees of intensity that Peirce assigns to sense-qualities and the degrees of vividness he assigns to ideas. In particular, primary colors achieve the highest degree of intensity and vividness, which is why the famous red sun, like the afterimage of a light flashed in the eye, glows in one's memory long after the page has been turned.

The same high pitch we saw in *Maggie* makes Crane's novel read like an expansion on Bacon: "a ciuill warre is as the heate of a feuer: but an honourable forraine warre is like the heate of exercise."[16] Thus "Pete swore redly" finds its equally expressionist counterpart in an outburst from the lieutenant: "'Come on. We'll all git killed if we stay here. We've on'y got t' go across that lot. And then—' The remainder of his idea disappeared in a blue haze of curses" (II, 107). The concluding phrase recalls the hazes that have gone before, such as "the blue haze of evening" (II, 71), not to mention the smoke, mists, and clouds metonymically evoked. Although it also recalls the Union blue, it strains from that phenomenal base toward a more expressionist extreme, spreading to the Lieutenant insofar as he comes to epitomize the martial spirit. This metonymic supplement, that is to say, draws from the phenomenal base that bears them while pulling away from that base by the *way* it draws. In the second chapter Wilson says to Henry, "'Yeh're gittin' blue, m' boy'" (II, 18); if this sense of the word also applies to the Lieutenant, then we have a soldier who, blue in dress, is also blue in attitude.

The movement from a phenomenal base to extremes is further illustrated by the case of the two crimsons. The first example, already discussed, is the crimson foam. The second reads: "The youth's reply was an outburst of crimson oaths" (II, 134). In the case of the foam, you will recall, the basic simile exploits a quasi-explicit likeness between the movement of the flags and the movement of waves, the modifier making the color of the foam match the color of the flags. Henry's crimson oath lacks a comparable base, no oath having a color in the way that any flag has. Rather, this crimson takes the temperature of Henry's outburst, which is hotter than that of the blue Lieutenant, giving it a register at once visual and emotional. It is not a long step from here to "Following this came a red rage" (II, 35). Though in this case there is no association as handy as bloody murder, red seems an appropriately choleric color, especially when the rage in question occurs on a battlefield.

In the following, Crane combines the reportorial with the "purely" expressive: "He was aware that these battalions ... were woven red and startling into the gentle fabric of softened greens and browns" (II, 24). Somewhat surprisingly, we do not see blue battalions, as might have been expected; they do not bear a color determination at all. This is because Crane is attending—from the color that belongs to the uniforms to the manner in which the army relates to the landscape, signified by an outburst of color, almost a tonal cry, that expressively gathers up associations with blood and war and heated emotions. In the quotation above, red as such is not present in the scene in the same reportorial way as greens and browns, it is rather a scenic distillation, a quintessence of the way in which the battalions become an aspect of the landscape, whose actual colors, shades, and tones would presumably be numerous, but which are at the same time essentialized into just two basic colors.

A more radical hypostasis occurs when color is attributed to an entirely imaginary phenomenon. Thus, after the phenomenally based colors in the book's opening passage, Jim comes back waving his shirt: "He adopted the important air of a herald and gold" (II, 3). The colors derive, in other words, not from the depicted presence of anything visual in either the landscape or the characters but by extrapolation from attitude, as in the "yellow discontent" of *Maggie*.

On a grander scale the final chapter offers this: "Regarding his procession of memory, he felt gleeful and unregretting, for, in it, his public deeds were paraded in great and shining prominence. Those performances which had been witnessed by his fellows marched now in wide purple and gold, hiding various deflections" (II, 133). Purple and gold are generic and abstract, counterparts of the intangible qualities of great and shining, which, without this translation into color, would want concreteness. In the manner of the imaginary herald, the process recorded here is attitudinal; it expresses the way the youth feels in relation to others and in relation to himself. In contrast to the earlier passage, the marching passage runs on considerably, as if to furnish by its length a quantitative complement to the expressive "exaggeration" of purple, with its splendor vaguely royal. In response to Wilson, whose probing could expose the truth of the red badge, Henry bursts out once more in crimson oaths; he then proceeds through an elaborate, seesawing process of self-justification until in the next-to-last paragraph he pronounces himself cured of "the red sickness of battle" (II, 135), whereupon "a golden ray of sun came through the hosts of leaden rain clouds" (II, 135). If this seems less radical than the imaginary procession of purple and gold, it is because Henry is trying to affirm the bond between himself and the world. To witness the color of the sun's ray as merely his own projection is far from his purpose. The ray must be more, it must in its very naturalness and immediacy represent the brightest and the best: no room here for the homeliness of "a yellow patch like a rug laid for the feet of the coming sun" (II, 15)—not when you can have the sun itself. Ultimately it is the transcendental, futural prospects of the sun that the color of the ray suggests. Higher than yellow, more precious and numinous, gold becomes in the final passage, like a yellow raised to its highest power, the color supreme.

There remains, finally, the use of the words *color* and *colors*. The latter, a companion term to flag, helps to keep visible the association between Henry and that symbol of his unit, the army as a whole, and victory. *Color*, the more significant term, can shade into *colors*, as when we are told that the color of the cloth indicates which side is winning. By metonymy the neutral term can take on a hue to which it is contiguous: "Here and there were flags, the red in the stripes dominating. They splashed bits of warm color upon the dark lines of troops" (II, 38). More often, color is a shorthand device to record a manifold of phenomena: "A thousand details of color and form surged in his mind" (II, 33).

Color is especially effective at making vivid whatever ineffable quality we feel to be the essence of something. Discussing love, Stendhal observes: "There is a physical cause, an incipient madness, a rush of blood to the brain, a disorder of the nervous system and the cerebral centres; compare the fleeting courage shown by stags and the color of a soprano's thoughts."[17] This use of the term lifts what is most basic and ownmost toward a more general level of articulation. This is no translation of the ineffable into the lucid: We do not hear the soprano's specific notes or the tone "colors" of her voice. The technique reveals immediately, evocatively, much as a whiff or a glance or a touch reveals—if not the thing itself we get at least the gist of it.

Closer to home, Whittier lets color signify that in ourselves from which we form compelling future patterns: "The tissue of the life to be / We weave with colors all our own."[18] For the Emerson of *Nature* colors signify those features of the human being that nature mediates, expressing them back to the spectator as its own delight: "Nature always wears the colors of the spirit. To a man laboring under calamity, the heat of his own fire hath sadness in it."[19] For the Thoreau of *Walden* a soldier's virtue has an innate color that, because it cannot indefinitely be concealed, need not be displayed: "nor need the soldier be so idle as to try to paint the precise *color* of his virtue on his standard. The enemy will find it out. He may turn pale when the trial comes."[20] Henry Fleming does more than turn pale when his trial begins; he fails it, at least at first; and all the while, in his own way, he is painting on the color of his virtue, as he would have it be perceived, the better to conceal his shame.

When Crane characterizes Henry's ambitions, he makes it clear that, as important as they may be, they are susceptible to change. The crucial statement occurs in the account of Mrs. Fleming's response to her son's desire to enlist: "At last, however, he had made firm rebellion against this yellow light thrown upon the color of his ambitions" (II, 6). In their original abstract state the ambitions warrant a comparably abstract noun, color; this, being indeterminate as to any specific hue or tone, leaves the nature of the ambitions open to the influence of anything that *is* specific, in the present case yellow light. If the yellow has here the contaminating effect for which Goethe's theory seeks to account, the colors in a later scene return to the phenomenal base, which is intensified, however, by the transcendent nature of the figure to whom they are applied: "[The flag] was a woman, red and white, hating and loving, that called him with the voice of his hopes" (II, 108).

Notes

15. Helpful discussions include Claudia C. Wogan, "Crane's Use of Color in *The Red Badge of Courage*," *Modern Fiction Studies* 6 (1960): 168–72; and Reid Maynard, "Red as Leitmotiv in *The Red Badge of Courage*," *American Quarterly* 30 (1974): 135–41.

16. *The Works of Francis Bacon*, ed. James Spedding, Robert Leslie Ellis, and Douglas Denon Heath (London: Longmans, 1870), VI, 588.

17. Stendhal, *Love*, trans. Gilbert and Suzanne Sale (Harmondsworth: Penguin, 1975), p. 60; *cf.* p. 59.

18. *The Poetical Works of John Greenleaf Whittier* (Boston: Houghton-Mifflin, 1892), II, 100.

19. Ralph Waldo Emerson, *Nature* (Boston: James Monroe, 1836), p. 14.

20. Henry David Thoreau, *Walden* (Harmondsworth: Penguin, 1983), p. 90.

DANIEL MARDER ON THE DESTRUCTION OF FLEMING'S ROMANTICISM

In *The Red Badge of Courage*, Crane penetrates the emotions that lie beneath the outer fact, Henry's fascination with the "immense and terrible machine" of battle. The dreamy greenhorn "must go close and see it produce corpses." Crane discarded the excessive coloring of the sketches of his earlier drafts; the "blazing sky" was too easy. Its language having been honed and streamlined over the successive drafts, the novel opens as an army awakens to a landscape changing from brown to green. A river, amber-tinted in the morning, turns sorrowfully black at night, but allows the gleam of red enemy camp-fires to be seen.

In *Maggie*, Crane not only explores the external forces that shape the lives of his characters, but, going beyond the merely environmental, also penetrates to human consciousness, the world we actually inhabit. He opens the inner life that determines what we see in the world. The novelist Hamlin Garland waxed on *Maggie*, "Egad, it has no style! Absolutely transparent! Wonderful—wonderful." Crane's grasp of emotions is even more apparent in the 18,000-word abridged newspaper version of *The Red Badge of Courage*. For Garland, who had slipped Crane fifteen dollars to retrieve the second half of the manuscript from the typist, the newspaper serial version was a work of "genius." But William Dean Howells, in a rare instance of misappraisal, remarked, "For me, I remain true to my first love, *Maggie*. That is better than all the *Black Riders* and *Red Badge*."

To write *The Red Badge of Courage*, Crane needed knowledge about the Civil War, and this he obtained by reading as much as he could on the subject. He pored over a series of articles in *Century Magazine*, titled "Battles and Leaders of the Civil War." He found the *Century* articles at the studio of his artist friend Corwin Knapp Linson, who had picked up the magazines in secondhand bookstores and kept them around for realistic examples of art. One article, "The Recollections of a Private," describes the act of enlisting and the flight at Bull Run. A second places the soldier in the woods after the battle; he touches the shoulder of another and realizes he is dead. Crane found these soldiers as "emotionless as rocks," but incorporated their experiences into his novel to great effect.

The serial version was released by the Bacheller-Johnson Syndicate in December 1894. It was carried by some 750 syndicated newspapers, in almost all cases, in six installments.

The New York Press printed the entire serial in its Sunday issue on December 9, 1894, while the six installments ran in *The Philadelphia Press* beginning December 3 and in *The Nebraska State Journal* beginning December 4. At the time of the serial's appearance, Crane was negotiating with D. Appleton and Company for publication of the book and, for obvious, self-serving reasons, denigrated the serial to Ripley Hitchcock, his future editor at Appleton, assuring him that "This is the war story in its syndicate form, that is to say, much smaller and to my mind much worse than its original form."

In October 1895, Appleton published the 50,000-word book, in which Crane restored most of the vital material he had cut for the serial. The 1895 publication of this "psychological portrait of fear" was an instant success. Crane looked upon his completed book as the triumph of a battle. Perhaps somewhat like Henry Fleming at the conclusion of the novel, he might have felt that he, too, had emerged "from the red sickness of battle ... and turned now with a lover's thirst to images of tranquil skies."

But in the novel, the quiet happiness of the end is not intended to be taken at face value. The "tranquil skies" are much too idyllic to be taken seriously. Whenever Henry is shocked or in low spirits, the sky seems to be against him; when he feels heroic, the sky is with him. The sky is directed precisely at Henry's capacity to feel it. Any divine concern for this pitiful soldier is as unsubstantiated as the belief that war is noble. Henry's facile views are destroyed by the realities of war; regardless of praise, Henry's inner knowledge of his feigned wound and of his desertion of the tattered soldier stays "near him always and darkens" his triumphant moment.

Readers of the serial do not have the opportunity to relive Henry's full experience. Entire episodes, such as Henry's conversations with his mother, are omitted. Contents of whole chapters (for example, Chapter XII, XV, and XVII) are either excised or compressed. Chapter IX in the serial is a reduced amalgam of Chapters IX and X, which manages to bury in the middle the famous simile, "The red sun was pasted in the sky like a fierce wafer." The omission of "fierce" from this line in the 1895 book further underscores nature's indifference to the tribulations of the regiment and to the war itself. The last three chapters of the book, which lend ambiguity to the ending, were all cut from the serial.

The serial is a far different story. Its pace is faster, and the blood and thunder of Henry's baptism of fire is more objective. At least in comparison to the novel, the slim volume seems overburdened with action; the removal of the philosophizing at various points in the narrative, while heightening the drama, somewhat skews the focus of the work. In its abridged state, the story is simpler and more direct, one of an inexperienced young man running towards self-redemption. Accordingly, the ironies of the novel are much fainter in the serial. But the serial version also provides strength to the novel. Severely cutting into Henry's ruminations, it puts greater emphasis on the immutability and indifference of the universe. Crane recognized this advantage and clung to this change as he went about preparing the manuscript for Appleton.

When later editors attempted to establish a "definitive" text for the novel, some reinserted text from his earlier drafts, material that Crane had deliberately excluded from the 1895 edition. For instance, the title line—"He wished that he too had a wound, a red badge of courage"—reads "... a little red badge of courage" in the serial; in an even earlier draft, the line originally read "... a little warm red badge of courage." By restoring text which Crane had eliminated, editors such as John Winterich, Robert Stallman, and Henry Binder have, in effect, taken it upon themselves to override Crane's own editorial decisions. Their "textually richer" editions are essentially regressive, leading the reader away from Crane's final intentions.

Works By Stephen Crane

Maggie: A Girl of the Streets (A New York Story), 1893.

The Black Riders and Other Lines, 1895.

The Red Badge of Courage: An Episode of the American Civil War, 1895.

George's Mother, 1896.

The Little Regiment and Other Episodes of the American Civil War, 1896.

The Third Violet, 1897.

The Open Boat and Other Tales of Adventure, 1898.

War Is Kind, 1899.

Active Service, 1899.

The Monster and Other Stories, 1899.

Whilomville Stories, 1900.

Wounds in the Rain: War Stories, 1900.

Great Battles of the World, 1901.

Last Words, 1902.

The O'Ruddy: A Romance (completed by Robert Barr), 1903.

Annotated Bibliography

Benfy, Christopher. *The Double Life of Stephen Crane*, New York: Alfred A. Knopf, 1992.

Benfy's biography makes the tantalizing claim that Crane imagined experiences, wrote about them, and *then* lived them, as opposed to what was typical of most of his contemporaries. The biography also looks at much of Crane's less famous work, the study of which in turn shows the influence of and on *The Red Badge of Courage*.

Earlier noted biographies by John Berryman (1950) and R. W. Stallman (1968) are now seen as flawed, and while Benfy's is not the definitive work (one has yet to emerge) his central claim makes it worth consideration.

Bradley, Sculley, ed., et al. *Stephen Crane's The Red Badge of Courage: An Authoritative Text, Backgrounds and Sources, Criticism*, New York: W. W. Norton and Company, 1976.

Offers extensive criticism of the book, highlights of which include a number of essays that have gone on to be included in other anthologies on Crane. Notable critics and writers represented here include Donald Pizer, John Berryman, Frank Norris, Joseph Conrad, and Edwin H. Cady.

Davis, Linda H. *Badge of Courage: The Life of Stephen Crane*, New York: Houghton Mifflin, 1998.

Though Davis's version of Crane's life offers little new information, it does make more use of the writer's correspondence than does Benfy's. It also makes use of scholarly work and apparatus (such as the Wertheim-Sorrentino Crane Log, q.v.) in enriching our understanding of the writer and his work.

Dooley, Patrick K. *The Pluralistic Philosophy of Stephen Crane*, Urbana: University of Illinois Press, 1993.

In arguing that Stephen Crane's writing was more than merely deterministic, Dooley examines the writer's fiction as well as the influence of Henry and William James and other nineteenth century philosophers to show how Crane's perception of reality accommodated pluralistic views of the world and experience. Further, Crane's realism underscored a multifaceted existence.

Gibson, Donald B. *The Red Badge of Courage: Redefining the Hero*, Boston: Twayne Publishers, 1988.

Gibson, Donald B. *The Fiction of Stephen Crane*, Carbondale: Southern Illinois University Press, 1968.

Two of the books that established Gibson's reputation as a Crane scholar, each takes a detailed look at Crane's fiction, the later volume concerning itself solely with *The Red Badge*. Gibson's earlier volume builds the case for Crane as a stylistic and thematic maverick, while the latter claims that Crane's novel divides the nineteenth century novelistic sensibility from that of the twentieth by its individualism, realism, harshness, and lack of romantic didacticism.

Halliburton, David. From *The Color of the Sky: A Study of Stephen Crane*, New York: Cambridge University Press, 1989.

Halliburton's volume considers the entire Crane opus in a sweeping volume, with numerous insights into *The Red Badge* and *Maggie*. Halliburton draws a number of conclusions, including linking Crane to a number of influential thinkers and writers (see Dooley, above), showing the importance of Crane's poetry to the rest of his work, and demonstrating that Crane's mastery of prosody contributed to the musical quality of his prose.

Mitchell, Lee Clark. *New Essays on* The Red Badge of Courage, New York: Cambridge University Press, 1986.

Just as do other entries in Cambridge's series of *New Essays*, the volume on Crane, edited by eminent American literature scholar Lee Clark Mitchell, contains essays spanning a variety of critical approaches to Crane's work.

Wertheim, Stanley and Paul Sorrentino. *The Crane Log: A Documentary Life of Stephen Crane 1871–1900*, New York: G.K. Hall & Co., 1994.

The same scholars who edited Crane's correspondence (producing a volume in 1988) followed their achievement with an exhaustive chronicling of the author's life, working to correct the numerous fallacies of R.W. Stallman's 1973 biography, and expanding on what little was available to John Berryman for his 1950 biography. Using manuscripts, diaries, correspondence, interviews, newspapers, and other documents, the scholars are able to log much of Crane's activity, by individual days, for much of the writer's life.

Robertson, Michael. *Stephen Crane, Journalism, and the Making of Modern American Literature*, New York: Columbia University Press, 1997.

Using Crane as the central writer in a study encompassing Ernest Hemingway, Henry James, Theodore Dreiser, William Dean Howells, and others, Robertson argues not only for the central importance of Crane's journalistic work to his novels, stories, and poems, but that Crane wrote during a period of changing attitudes toward journalism generally. Furthermore, Robertson argues that consideration of Crane's journalism elevates it rightly to the level of literary journalism.

Contributors

Harold Bloom is Sterling Professor of the Humanities at Yale University. He is the author of 30 books, including *Shelley's Mythmaking, The Visionary Company, Blake's Apocalypse, Yeats, A Map of Misreading, Kabbalah and Criticism, Agon: Toward a Theory of Revisionism, The American Religion, The Western Canon*, and *Omens of Millennium: The Gnosis of Angels, Dreams, and Resurrection. The Anxiety of Influence* sets forth Professor Bloom's provocative theory of the literary relationships between the great writers and their predecessors. His most recent books include *Shakespeare: The Invention of the Human*, a 1998 National Book Award finalist; *How to Read and Why; Genius: A Mosaic of One Hundred Exemplary Creative Minds; Hamlet: Poem Unlimited; Where Shall Wisdom Be Found?*; and *Jesus and Yahweh: The Names Divine*. In 1999, Professor Bloom received the prestigious American Academy of Arts and Letters Gold Medal for Criticism. He has also received the International Prize of Catalonia, the Alfonso Reyes Prize of Mexico, and the Hans Christian Andersen Bicentennial Prize of Denmark.

Gabriel Welsch's short stories, poems, and reviews have appeared in *Georgia Review, Mid-American Review, Crab Orchard Review*, and *Cream City Review*. He regularly reviews literature for *Harvard Review, Missouri Review, Slope*, and *Small Press Review*. He received a Pennsylvania Council on the Arts Fellowship for Literature in fiction in 2003.

Christopher Benfey is Mellon Professor of English at Mount Holyoke College. His volumes of criticism include *Degas in New Orleans, Emily Dickinson and the Problem of Others*, and *The Great Wave: Gilded Age Misfits, Japanese Eccentrics, and the Opening of Old Japan*.

Linda H. Davis is a biographer whose books include *Onward and Upward: A Biography of Katharine White, Badge of Courage: The Life of Stephen Crane*, and *Charles Addams: A Cartoonist's Life*.

Ben Satterfield has taught at the University of Texas, and has published in numerous journals, including *Studies in American Fiction, Southwest Review, Oxford Magazine*.

Donald E. Pease is Professor of English and Avalon Foundation Chair of the Humanities at Dartmouth College. Among his numerous publications are *The American Renaissance Reconsidered: Selected Papers of the English Institute, 1982–1983, New Americanists: Revisionist Interventions into the Canon*, and *Futures of American Studies*.

Kevin J. Hayes is professor of English at the University of Central Oklahoma and the author of several books, including *Poe and the Printed Word* and *An American Cycling Odyssey, 1887*.

David Halliburton is the author of *Edgar Allan Poe, Poetic Thinking: An Approach to Heidegger, The Color of the Sky: A Study of Stephen Crane*, and *The Fateful Discourse of Worldly Things*. He is Professor Emeritus of English, Comparative Literature, and Modern Thought at Stanford University.

Alfred Kazin (1915-1998) was the author of several books, including *New York Jew, An American Procession, A Writer's America, A Lifetime Burning in Every Moment*, and *God and the American Writer*. While he was a prominent New Critic and member of the "New York Intellectuals," for many Kazin's greatest contribution was his memoirs of the immigrant experience.

Daniel Marder is a retired Professor of English at the University of Tulsa.

Giorgio Mariani teaches American literature at the University of Rome, and is the author of *Spectacular Narratives: Representations of Class and War in Stephen Crane and the American 1890s* and *Post-Tribal Epics: The Native American Novel Between Tradition and Modernity*.

Lee Clark Mitchell is Holmes Professor of Belles-Lettres and Professor of English at Princeton University. His numerous books include *Determined Fictions: American Literary Naturalism*, *Westerns: Making the Man in Fiction and Film*, and *The Photograph and the American Indian*.

Acknowledgments

"Introduction" by Lee Clark Mitchell. From *New Essays on* The Red Badge of Courage, Cambridge University Press, 1986, pp. 16–19. © 1986 by Cambridge University Press. Reprinted by permission.

"Image and Emblem in *The Red Badge of Courage*" by Kevin J. Hayes. From *Writers and Their Work: Stephen Crane*, Northcote House Publishers, 2004, pp. 40–44. © 2004 by Northcote House. Reprinted by permission.

"Crane's Writing Is Disappointing" by Alfred Kazin. From *Readings on Stephen Crane*, ed. Bonnie Szumski, Greenhaven Press, 1998, pp. 34–38. Originally published as chapter 2 of *On Native Ground: An Interpretation of Modern American Prose Literature*. © 1942 and renewed 1970 by Alfred Kazin. Reprinted by permission.

"The Private War" by Christopher Benfy. From *The Double Life of Stephen Crane*, Alfred A. Knopf, 1992, pp. 108–119. © 1992 by Christopher Benfy. Reprinted by permission.

"The Parsonage: The Noise of Rumors" by Linda H. Davis. From *Badge of Courage: The Life of Stephen Crane*, Houghton Mifflin, 1998, pp. 68–71. © 1998 by Linda H. Davis. Reprinted by permission.

"From Romance to Reality: The Accomplishment of Private Fleming," by Ben Satterfield. From *CLA Journal* vol. XXIV, no. 4 (June 1981): pp. 451–453.

"Fear, Rage, and the Mistrials of Representation in *The Red Badge of Courage*," by Donald Pease. From *American Realism: New Essays*, Eric J. Sundquist, ed. (Baltimore and London: The Johns Hopkins University Press, 1982): pp. 155–157.

Index